Moving Toward Stillpoint

A Mother's Transformational Journey with Her Dying Son

By Therese Luce

To Ilene,
Life is a transforming journey
for each of us. Blessings on
yours. Thank you for
allowing me to share mine
with you. Gratefully,
Therese Luce

Grateful acknowledgment is made to the following for permission to reprint previously published material:

Here I Am Lord, Text and Music by Daniel L. Schutte © 1981, OCP PUBLICATIONS, 5536 NE HASSALO, PORTLAND, OR 97213. ALL RIGHTS RESERVED. USED WITH PERMISSION.

MBB Inc., excerpt from *Life After Life,* used by written permission from Raymond A. Moody, Jr., M.D.

University of Notre Dame Press: Excerpt from *Light of the Night* by Jean-Francois Six, translated by John Bowden from the French. 1998 English Edition published in the USA by University of Notre Dame Press, Notre Dame, IN 46556. Used by permission.

Random House Inc. Excerpt from *A Path With Heart,* by Jack Kornfield.

The author gratefully acknowledges permission to quote Terese Fabbri, Deacon Ray Gartner, and family members.

Cover art by Janet Jaffke (jjaffke@comcast.net)
Page layout and pre-press services by Sally Elvart (SallyElvart@hotmail.com)

ISBN 0-9769411-0-4
978-0-9769411-0-1

Printed in the United States of America

To purchase additional copies, reprint permissions, or other information write to Stillpoint, P.O. Box 132, New Buffalo, Michigan 49117 or e-mail: tgl425@comcast.net

This book is dedicated to Christopher – our son, brother, friend, teacher

*"But the souls of the just are in the hands of God,
and no torment shall touch them.
They seem in the view of the foolish to be dead;
and their passing away was thought an affliction,
and their going forth from us, utter destruction.
But they are in peace."*

Wisdom 3: 1-3

❧ Acknowledgments ❧

Most efforts of the heart and spirit would not be possible without the support and encouragement of significant others. This work is no exception. I am grateful to so many for so much. I wish to thank my husband Jack for his encouragement, understanding, and patience during the long years that we grieved for our son and I attempted to write about our experience. His support made it possible for me to walk once again through the memories and the pain of that last year and a half.

My special love and thanks to my children Maryann, Michele, and John who, no less than Chris, have been the joys of my life and my true teachers. I will always be grateful to our sons-in-law David, Steve, and Doug for their caring presence. I thank God for my grandchildren David, Nicole, Jenna, Dominic, and Aidan who bring laughter into my life and joy to my heart.

I thank my parents Sam and Mary, my sisters Joanne and Angie and their families for their sustained support, love, and prayers.

I thank my daughters Maryann and Michele, my mother-in-law Mary, and my son-in-law Doug for sharing their visions of Christopher with me. My special thanks to my son John who has given me advice, encouragement, and unconditional support. During the last seventeen years many people have shared their stories with me. Their experiences along with ours convinced me that our loved ones who have died wish us to know that they continue to participate in our lives.

Thanks also to my special friend Terese who inspired, nurtured, and directed me in my spiritual journey. I thank my dear friends Sharon and Kathy for their empathy and their ability to listen. I am grateful to Father Jim for his spiritual insights, for his editorial assistance, and for encouraging me to "dance my dance." I'm grateful to Sally for her diligence in preparing the manuscript for printing, thanks to Janet for her creative cover illustration, and special thanks to Mary for her help with the editing. I extend my gratitude to readers Juanita, Ruth Ann, Diane, Carol, Vivian, Joanne, Ange, Kathy, and Maryann for their encouragement, and insights. Special thanks to my spiritual "sisters" Eden, Maryann, Carol, Sue, Judy, and Gail.

I will always be grateful to Dr. Eldon Ruff, Dr. Vince Peterson, and Dr. Tom Trotter, professors in the Masters Counseling program at Indiana University, South Bend. Their support and encouragement before and after Chris's death helped me to finish the last year and a half of graduate work and to begin to write this book.

I wish to thank all of the medical and hospital personnel who helped Chris, especially Doctors Hemmy, Anderson, Pejic, and McDonald, and Saint Anthony Hospital. Thanks to all of our friends, our parish family, Father Bertino, Father Dettmer, and the countless people of many faiths, who prayed for Chris and for our family. Their gift of prayer sustained and nurtured us during Chris's illness and long after his death. Last but not least, I am very thankful for the guidance given by the angels and guides who support and nurture us in our earthly efforts.

⁊ℒ PREFACE ⅔ᛊ

I began to write this book shortly after my son, Christopher's death in response to a need to write about the journey that he set in motion when at age twenty-two he was diagnosed with the worst of the kidney-cell cancers, hypernephroma. He lived the last seven of the nineteen months that he was ill, in a hospital bed in the family room as a paraplegic. I perceive those nineteen months as a physical, emotional, and spiritual journey that my family and I took with Chris. I'd like to share that journey with you, and tell you what it was like to be Chris's mother during those months that I took care of him.

When Chris was stricken with cancer it was a shock that disrupted every aspect of our lives, our ideas about who we thought we were, our plans and dreams for the future, our relationships, and our work. We were faced with confusing and mind-numbing choices about medical treatments. We became more acutely aware of death and its proximity. We knew fear, rage, despair, and grief. Why was it then that we learned the most during that time? I believe it was because during that period when our lives seemed to have shattered in a thousand pieces, we became open to change, to possibility, to deeper love, and to developing and drawing from our own personal strength. Most importantly we became aware of the mystery surrounding our lives and open to understanding that each soul has a plan for its own life.

I completed the main body of this book within a year of Chris's death. In the ensuing years, I embarked on a slow and steady process of going over each page, clarifying and developing my thoughts. The process opened me to many new insights. Had I completed the work immediately after Chris's death, it would have focused on Chris's emotional and physical suffering, and the pain and heartache that we, his family, experienced as a result of his illness. Pain and grief are still present, but now, years later, I see things from a broader perspective. In 1987 I would have written from the perspective of what my husband, Jack and I, and our children, Maryann, Michele, and John did for Chris. Now, I understand that Chris did much more for us than we did for him. Being present to his physical, emotional, and spiritual suffering changed our lives. What we witnessed was not a miracle of healing, but one of transformation. Because, as Chris lost physical abilities, he grew in non-physical qualities: remarkable courage, endurance, patience, wisdom, faith in God, and enduring love. We learned so much about life, love, and eternity through the painful journey that we took with Christopher.

More importantly, our story did not end when Chris died. Our relationship with Chris did not end when we buried him. He has been able to make his presence known in many ways and many times in the years since his death. For reasons unknown to my family and me, Chris has been allowed to continue to participate in our lives. I believe that after his transition, he asked and was granted permission to continue to be present to us. In so doing he has taught us that we do not lose those we love when they make the transition to the next life. They continue to love and care about us, and sometimes, like Chris they are able to make their presence known. Our experiences have been validated by writers like Atlea, Puryear, Moody, Kubler-Ross, and Van Praagh.

This surely is the good news for us all. Although this is a story about losing our young son to cancer, it is more than that. It is a story that speaks of learning to love more deeply, of learning to live more authentically, of deeper faith and trust in God, of spiritual growth, and of hope and belief in life after death. These are the gifts that I wish to share with the reader, especially with those who are caring for loved ones and are being stretched to the limit of their abilities; because it is an exciting story of hope and unending love.

I did much soul searching about what this book should

encompass. Should I exclude the personal, intimate parts of our lives? Should I include excerpts from my journal - writing that exposed my deepest emotional state? Should I reveal my spiritual beliefs and experiences, and recount the occasions when my family and I have seen or in some way experienced Chris's presence? My decision to include all of it was based finally on the principle that to exclude any part of it would be to omit part of the truth of my experience. The purpose then of this book is to openly and honestly share with you the journey that started on October 17, 1985.

❧ CONTENTS ❧

✥ 1 ✥

PAIN AND MISPLACED TRUST

"Dad, I have a pain that is so severe that it knocked me to my knees. The Emergency Room doctor doesn't know what's causing it. He told me to call my parents and see my family physician. Could you and Mom come and get me."

We would not know until four months later how those words were to forever change our lives. So on that Thursday night at 10:00 p.m. equipped with pillows, blankets, and pain pills, my husband Jack and I drove to Purdue University where Chris was a junior and brought him home.

Chris had transferred to Purdue after completing two and a half years at Wabash College. Although he loved and thrived on the intellectual challenge of his Wabash classes, in January of 1985, he transferred to Purdue in order to pursue his first love – building construction. There he moved into the Delta chapter of Phi Kappa Psi where he was immediately befriended, accepted as a brother and elected historian. In spring he was elected house manager of the fall term and had been asked to run for vice-president the following year. Purdue was for Chris the culmination of a life-long dream. He was in a field he loved, he was flying through his courses, and he was making new friends. After two semesters he was eagerly looking forward to the challenge of graduate school.

The atmosphere suited Chris perfectly. He had left the male atmosphere of Wabash and now was thoroughly enjoying the weekend party atmosphere of the campus. His white Honda CRX was his pride and joy and gave him the freedom to date now that he seemed to be getting over the breakup with the girl he had dated for three years.

His Sunday night calls from school would last half an hour as he enthusiastically talked about his classes, his new fraternity brothers, and the girls he was meeting. He said he loved his life. He loved his life so much that during that fall semester of 1985, when he started having pain, he continued to carry 21 hours, to be house manager, to direct the pledges as they worked on house repairs, to date, and to enjoy fraternity life.

All his fun came crashing to a halt on February 6, 1986, when the head of urology at a university medical center informed us that Chris's pain was caused by a cancerous mass on his kidney. But on that fateful Thursday night in October when we went to Purdue to bring him home we knew none of this.

Jack, a physician, thought the location of Chris's pain indicated a kidney problem. So early the next morning, Jack took Chris to the hospital to see urologist and long time friend and colleague, Dr. Tom Smith (fictitious name). Dr. Smith, too, thought it could be a kidney stone and ordered an IV pyelogram of the kidney. Upon looking at the test results, Dr. Smith said it was probably a stone. The left kidney was functioning, but not as well as the right kidney. The decision was made to perform a retrograde pyelogram on Monday if Chris did not pass a stone at home over the weekend.

Chris continued to have severe pain during the weekend. He faithfully filtered his urine for stones, but to our disappointment he didn't pass any. It would have been a relief if kidneys stones were the problem, because there would be an easy solution.

On Monday morning we took him to the hospital and a retrograde pyelogram was performed. After the procedure, Dr. Smith came into the surgery lounge and with a look of surprise said, "There were no stones."

I was disturbed by his statement. Doubt. With so much pain, there had to be a reason. I felt the familiar anxiety and fear, the ones that always crept in whenever one of my children was ill. Those were times that interrupted the ordinary flow and routine of my life, demanding to be noticed, reminding me of life's fragility. I chided myself that this was not a new experience for me, having been a mother for twenty seven years. And so reason took over, quashed my anxiety, and reminded me that medicine had never failed us before. It was all self-talk compressed into a moment. And so I simply responded to Dr. Smith with, "What else could be causing the pain?"

Without hesitation, he said, "non-opaque kidney stones."

Wanting to believe him, I asked, "What can be done about those."

He replied, "They don't show up and they are not visible."

He didn't seem concerned or suggest that the pain could have another cause, and he didn't suggest that any further tests be run. He further added that perhaps minerals in the water at Crawfordsville and Lafayette, where Chris had spent the past three years, were conducive to the formation of stones.

Upon hearing the diagnosis, Chris said if that were the case, he would rest for a few hours and drive back to school. With his heavy schedule, he didn't want to waste any more time away from school.

I disagreed. I thought we should look into this a little further and discuss other options. But Chris was adamant and Jack agreed with Chris, and I backed down. I will forever regret not insisting on another opinion. If there were a moment I could live over it would be that one, because the delay of four and a half months did irreparable harm to Chris's chance for recovery. I learned the hard way that I must listen to my gut feeling, my intuition.

I should add at this point that Jack, who is a specialist in ob/gyn never thought to question Dr. Smith's diagnostic judgment in his field of expertise. But it was more than simply respect for medical judgment. Jack and I had been similarly raised in families and parochial schools where respect for authority and compliance had been ingrained upon us. Such an environment does little to foster confidence in one's innate ability to discern.

We will forever regret that decision. Trust must be coupled with common sense. No one has all the answers all of the time.

Doctors are not infallible, not even well trained ones. We should immediately have gone to one of the university centers in Chicago for a second opinion despite Chris's protests.

Instead Chris went back to school to endure continued pain. For the rest of that fall semester, he continued to attend classes, have a social life, be house manager supervising work that needed to be done - in spite of the pain. Jack and I were both concerned about the persistence of the pain. When we spoke to him once or twice a week we'd ask him if the pain had subsided. He said he was still hurting, but he dismissed it as though he was learning to live with it.

The pain was still there. It was a big clue, but to our eternal regret, we didn't pick up on it. Our attention was focused on all the exciting events that were taking place in our family. Maryann, our oldest child and her husband Dave, both physicians in training, were expecting their first child, our first grandchild in November. John, a business consultant, had been sent to work in London for three months; Michele would graduate in January and we were planning a party, and I was realizing my own dream of graduate school. The year before, I had entered a Master's in counseling program and I was very absorbed in the work I was doing.

I had had a brief teaching career that ended when our second daughter, Michele was born, quickly followed by John and Chris. Caring for our children became my priority. Although I was pleased that my husband was in the helping profession there was a down side to being an obstetrician's family. The responsibility of raising four active children had essentially been mine. With four children to chauffeur, like many mothers, I became "my mother the car." I spent so much time behind the wheel driving children to school, sports, guitar and dance lessons that I wondered whether the teamsters union would expect me to pay dues for all the hauling I was doing.

Now they were in their twenties and pursuing their own careers. Jack and I were enjoying the freedom and the fruits of seeing our children grown up and becoming independent, and now that he had two partners, we had more time together. Life was good. So at this point in my life, I felt entitled to go after something that I had wanted for a long time. I had raised the children and been there for them, it was my turn to concentrate on my own goals.

I had finally grown out of my family of origin role of being compliant, nonassertive – my dreams don't matter kind of person into one who was entitled to pursue what she wanted. I felt self assured and capable of meeting the challenge of graduate school, and proud of my assertiveness. I remember thinking, "This is for me; nothing will stop me from completing this degree." That was before Chris became ill. A different era. I have heard it said that, "If you want to hear God laugh, tell him your plans for your life." God certainly must have had a good chuckle when he heard my plan.

One Friday morning in November Chris called to say he couldn't stand the pain any longer. I quickly drove down to pick him up. If Chris said he was in great pain, I believed him. He seemed to have an enormous tolerance for pain, having endured more than his share in his short life, including ligation of varicose veins and removal of an osteochondroma from his cervical spine.

It seemed I had always worried about Chris, all the way back to before he was born. I remember how relieved I was when the nurse put the little bundle of life in my arms and I looked down on my fourth child and second son who decided to enter the world on the last day of the year, 1963. He was wrapped mummy-like in imitation of the warm womb he had just left, so only his round, pink, blotchy little face was visible. His lashless eyelids were puffy and swollen, and sprouts of straight black hair went every which way on his little head. I eased the blanket away so I could touch his sweet fingers and see for myself that he was perfect. I kissed his soft pudgy cheek and simply looked at him.

My forth child – and yet, I experienced the same scary and awesome feeling that I had had when holding each of my babies for the first time. This fragile new life was totally dependent on me! He was in my hands – to care for, to love, to nurture, to teach. God had given me this little life and I was both intimidated and overwhelmed by the enormity of the gift and the responsibility of caring for him. And yet the commitment was instantaneous.

Although he and I had been together for nine months, I didn't know him. Our relationship was just beginning. For now he was a little stranger with a pink expressionless face. But soon his every smile and nuance would captivate me, and I would fall in love with him as I had with each of my children. For now he was a blank page, an empty floppy disc, or so I thought. I was deceived by the smallness of the package. Little did I know then that, like each of us, he had a purpose, a sacred task to fulfill. And little did I know that, like each of us, he was given the perfect life situation in which to accomplish that task.

I was tired and groggy, but I felt an inner joy and contentment as I continued to gaze at the little guy in my arms. What a relief to finally see and hold him. I had worried for months that there would be something wrong with him, and I prayed daily that he would be born healthy. After a long, hard pregnancy I whispered thank you to God for answering our prayers. I had been taking medication to relieve gall bladder attacks. Although I stopped taking all medication when I learned that I was pregnant; I was terrified that even taking them for those first few weeks would have an impact on the baby's health. Jack too was relieved that our baby was healthy. Although he kept reassuring me that the baby would be fine, he had silently worried that something would be wrong.

Christopher. No, Christopher Gerard in honor of St. Gerard, patron saint of pregnant women. After many years of thinking Gregory, the name Christopher came to me out of the blue a few weeks before his birth. Since he was going to be a Christmas baby, due to arrive on the 29th of December, the name seemed appropriate to both Jack and me. We said the name out loud and repeated it several times, Christopher. Now, as I looked at him, I knew for sure. Yes, he was definitely Christopher, Christ bearer. I wouldn't know until twenty-two years later just how appropriate the name would be.

I held him so that his heart was close to mine, and I could feel his fuzzy head under my chin, and feel his breathe on my neck, and I day dreamed of what he would become. A writer. A name like Christopher Luce was perfect for a writer. I pictured him at a typewriter – intelligent, serious, wearing a sweater, with a pipe in his mouth pounding out a great novel. If only mothers had that much control over their children's lives.

Jack was delighted to have a second son especially now that he was in the Navy with regular hours that allowed him time to participate in the life of our family. We were relieved, happy and grateful to have him, and anxious to bring him home to his two older sisters, Maryann, almost six, Michele, four and a half, and brother, John, almost three. It was a perfect family – two girls and two boys.

On our arrival the kids greeted me with hugs and kisses, jumping up and down eager to get a peak at the little blanket wrapped bundle. Their eyes grew wide with awe as they surrounded him on the bed giggling delightedly, touching his little fingers, giving him gentle kisses, taking turns holding their new baby brother.

But Chris was not a contented baby as our other three infants had been. He cried often after eating, pulling up his little legs as though he had cramps. I'd hold and snuggle him, but it was hard to soothe him. I took him to the pediatrician who examined him and pronounced him well. "Some babies are just finicky," he said. But I knew there was a problem. Like a sore tooth, it was always there getting my attention. Was the medication that I had taken during those early weeks of my pregnancy the cause? I wonder to this day if that was the precipitating cause of his future health problems.

When Chris was six months old, Jack finished his two years of naval service and we moved back to the Midwest so that we could be close to our families. We relocated, Jack joined a medical practice, and I found a new pediatrician. But the problem still went undiagnosed. In spite of my repeated complaints to the first two pediatricians that there must be something wrong with Chris, they simply treated him for whatever problem he was having at the time and never delved any further.

He had stopped crying after eating but other problems developed. He often had diarrhea, and he caught all the contagious diseases that his siblings brought home from school. His skin became a canvas for measles, roseola, German measles, and mumps. It seemed that every week our poor baby was sick with something, a cold or a fever, or a contagious disease. His little body suffered the effects because he wasn't gaining as much weight as he should. His face was often flushed and blotchy, and his tummy was distended. I worried constantly as did Jack. Jack had no experience with infants after they were delivered, so he too deferred to the expert, our pediatrician. To our utter regret, we were to make this error in judgment again.

I worried continuously. I kept repeating, "There has to be a problem; this isn't normal for an infant." Why was Chris always sick? Yet the only problem ever addressed was the immediate one. It took eighteen months and another move to finally, finally find a pediatrician who heard me. By this time Chris was eighteen months old, weighed eighteen pounds, and looked malnourished. Dr. Bob who attended lectures every week at children's Hospital listened attentively as I recounted a litany of Chris's illnesses. He immediately ordered a battery of tests to determine the underlying cause. Thank God, at last someone who understood – the answer to my prayers.

The tests revealed that Chris had an allergy to fat found primarily in the milk he drank. What a relief not only to know what the problem was, but also to be offered a solution. Once

Chris was put on skim milk and all fat was completely eliminated from his diet, he gained weight, and began to thrive. When
Dr. Bob said he would eventually outgrow the allergy my anxiety abated, but tucked into a corner of my mind was the fear
that his start in life had been compromised by the medication I
had taken. Later on that niggling fear surfaced whenever Chris
had a tummy ache. Consequently, if he asked to stay home
from school that day, I let him, even though I sometimes
thought he just needed down time. He was an A student like
his siblings, so I gave him the benefit of the doubt. My fear also
surfaced on occasions when he'd complain that he didn't like
what we were having for dinner. If it was possible, I'd fix him
something else. Of course, our other kids thought he was
spoiled. In the ensuing years I sometimes would remember his
early difficulties and worry that he would have a recurring
problem later in life. I just didn't know how devastating the
problem would be.

In spite of the shaky start in life, Chris was a good baby and
his illnesses had not slowed down his physical development.
He crawled, stood, and walked before he was a year old. And he
was bright. I have an image of Chris as a toddler flushed from
sleep, with tousled hair, wearing a floppy, yellow, one piece
sleeper, waddling along the upstairs hall, then laying down on
his tummy, backing up to the top of the stairs, straightening his
body, sliding all the way down on his tummy, them standing up
at the bottom with a big grin of accomplishment on his face.

He developed a sense of fairness early on. Being the little guy
he had to put up with his brother and sisters playing tricks on
him. The older three would pretend to fight and end up in a
dog pile on the floor. Without any fear, he would fly into the
middle of the fray pushing and pulling at the ones on top so
that he could rescue who ever was on the bottom. It was a
game that worked until the little three-year-old caught on.
What it did for Chris was to teach him empathy and fair play.
He would side with whom ever was at a disadvantage or losing

an argument, especially among his siblings. Later, on the play ground he could defend himself when necessary, but he wasn't mean or spiteful.

At four, he was energetic and inquisitive, and loved to play with anything he could take apart and put back together. He'd sit cross legged on the floor working on erector sets, surrounded with parts, contented, absorbed, and focused. As with pieces of a puzzle, he would patiently try to fit one piece into another until he found the right one. As he developed fine motor skills, we bought progressively harder sets to challenge his growing ability. He'd work, head bent over a project consulting the diagram until he got it. No complaint that a project was too hard, no giving up in frustration. Consequently, he was never bored; nor needed to be entertained, because he would always find an activity that he liked. That early training taught him tenacity and self reliance.

Now on the drive home from Purdue, tenacity and determination were very much in evidence, because in spite of the pain, Christopher could talk of nothing but how exciting it was to be at Purdue, and to be part of the program he was in. He was looking forward to graduating and pursuing a Master's degree. He thought he also might want to get a real estate broker's license to tie in with his building construction major, because he wanted to become a real estate entrepreneur. I marveled at our son who was in so much pain that he had to be driven home from school on a Friday morning, and still was so excited about his wonderful plans for his future that he could speak of nothing else.

Jack had set up an appointment to see Dr. Smith. X-rays were repeated, and again, Dr. Smith said nothing was visible. Chris, Jack, and I were stymied, but since Dr. Smith expressed no concern, we again mistakenly put our trust in his opinion. Chris returned to school the next day because he had so much work to do. During November and December I encountered Dr. Smith a couple of times, and told him Chris was still in a lot of pain. Again he said, "Non-opaque stones, tell him to drink cranberry juice." Then he quickly started talking about golf. He completely dismissed the problem Chris was having. At our second encounter he again dismissed Chris's pain as not important. Looking back, it seems insane that we never even considered the possibility that he was wrong. We trusted him completely, without doubt. To our last day we will regret not tempering trust with sound judgment.

In December, Christopher called to say he had pain in his testicles. He came home to see Dr. Smith again. Dr. Smith did not say there was any relationship between the problem with the kidney and the painful testicles. He thought that a blood vessel close to the surface of the testicle might be the problem. It might have to be removed if it didn't quiet down because it could cause Chris to become sterile at some point. He told Chris to apply ice packs whenever he was lying down. During December whenever Chris was not in class he would lie down in his bed and apply an ice pack to his groin.

Chris came home for the Christmas holidays but he did not complain of pain, although he must have lived with it. He was quieter but he did spend time with friends and even went on an overnight ski trip with his fraternity brothers but he did not ski.

In January Chris drove in with his friend to attend Michele's Graduation party. He was very thin. He could not eat a lot because he was having so much pain. Again, I asked him to come home but he said no; after the party he and Todd intended to make the three-hour drive back to school. Months later, after his surgery, he told me he needed to bring a friend because he was afraid of driving alone while in so much pain.

On January 30th, Chris called early in the morning to say he couldn't stand the pain any more, could he come home. He said the painful testicle was now swollen and this was causing more pain. He said he would drive himself home. By the time he arrived home he had blood in his urine. Jack made an appointment with Dr. Smith. It was the doctor's day off, but he told Jack to bring Chris to his home where he could take a look at him. He examined him standing up in his lower level family room. They told me afterwards that the doctor jokingly said that it was probably due to his not having enough sex. Again he said there was nothing wrong. He did not put him into the hospital; he didn't see the need for more tests.

Chris stayed until Saturday morning. But he said he had to get back to school. He looked terrible. He said to me, "Mom what are we going to do?"

I called the doctor and asked, "What should we do; he's in so much pain."

He said, "Tell him to drink cranberry juice because he is forming non opaque stones. He needs to bring cranberry juice back to school with him. He continued, "When the pain stops we will do more tests." When the pain stops!!

Before he left Chris and I went to the store and bought eight gallons of cranberry juice. He walked around very carefully. As I drove, we talked. I knew he was in bad shape. When we returned he got back into his car and drove back to school.

I look back at those three and a half months and I am heartbroken and appalled that I didn't insist in October that we get a second opinion, have more tests done, go somewhere else to have the tests read? Why didn't the three of us sit down and talk about all these possibilities? Maybe if I had had a temper tantrum or screamed or yelled or did whatever it took to get him to stay home, I might have gotten Chris to listen, gotten somebody to listen. I will regret my passivity for the rest of my life. Why didn't any of us question Dr. Smith's judgment? Perhaps it is because we expect that a specialist is an expert in his field and always makes a correct diagnosis. How irresponsible we were! Couldn't I have learned to listen to my inner voice, my gut feeling without such a devastating lesson? I did have an inner voice that said something was wrong. I kept putting it down, deferring to Dr. Smith, because certainly he knew more than I did. Jack too was full of remorse that he allowed his common sense and good judgment to be colored by an "expert opinion."

Early Tuesday morning, the 4th of February, Christopher called again to say he couldn't stand it any longer, could he come home. We said, of course. Did he need a ride? No, he would drive home himself.

I told Jack we had to call in someone else and Jack quickly agreed. It was the week that Dr. Smith was away on vacation. I wonder if we would have had the common sense to call in someone else anyway, but I don't know. That week we had no recourse except to find someone else.

❧ 2 ❧

THE DEVASTATING TRUTH

D r. Peters (fictitious name) the head of urology at a university hospital in Chicago, upon hearing his symptoms gave Chris an appointment for the next day. That morning at the hospital while waiting for Chris to complete a series of tests, I took a few minutes to write in my journal. Whenever I reread the entry I made that morning, I am struck by the shallowness of my thoughts. I seemed to be involved with "taking my own pulse." It was another time, a time before my whole focus would be on Christopher.

Journal Entry • February 6, 1986

I'm not handling stress very well. Chris's illness has been a recurring problem. I'm now at the hospital in Chicago waiting for Chris and the results of the arteriogram. I am not centered. I'm worried. My body feels heavy, rather numb; my movements are slow and jerky. I feel jittery. I know my face feels and looks long, thin, and drawn. My eyes are lifeless, dull and opaque. Periodically, I take deep, heaving breaths. My stomach is burning. Surprisingly, my jaw is not clenched, but slack; my neck muscles are relaxed. I guess when I am in deep tension and stress, my body is so limp and heavy that it becomes relaxed, and all the tension becomes internalized within my stomach and in paralyzing self-talk. I'm praying. I went to Mass. I've said a rosary to the Holy Spirit and I prayed to St. Jude, hope of hopeless cases. I've blessed Chris and myself and prayed to the Blessed Mother. I am praying that the Lord's will for Chris is to be free of malignancy. In Jesus name I have asked. I will stop writing, I need to hold my rosary and pray.

I said my prayers and even though I thought of malignancy, I did not really believe that it could be cancer. In the back of my mind I knew that Chris did not have that terrible thing. After all, medicine had always been able to cure us of any and all of our physical problems. I had had several serious surgeries and I had always recovered quickly and completely. Whenever any of our children had had any health problems we could always count on medicine to make them well. We were a medical family; we had seen the "miracles" that modern medicine performed. We trusted it. It had always worked in the past and it would work for Chris now.

We returned to Chris's room to wait for him. Jack, seeing Chris's chart on the desk, read it and blanched. I tried to get him to talk to me but he could not seem to form the words. Finally he blurted, "There's a mass." I was in denial because I could not comprehend what he meant. It never occurred to me that it was a tumor or a cancerous mass, even though I had written about it in my journal a couple of hours before.

Finally, at two in the afternoon, Chris was wheeled in. He was relieved that the tests were over. Yes, he was in pain. The three of us anxiously waited until Dr. Peters finished office hours and could tell us the results. In the meantime, a radiology resident phoned Chris with a request that he undergo a new procedure called an MRI at no cost to us or to our insurance company. He explained that Chris's diagnosis by way of the arteriogram could be used to test whether the MRI came up with the same diagnosis. Chris explained to him that he did not know whether he would need surgery, or how long he would need to be in the hospital, because his doctor had not been in to tell him the result of the arteriogram. The resident assured him that he would be having surgery. Sadly, that was how we learned that Chris would have to undergo surgery.

Dr. Peters, the urologist, came in with a fixed smile on his face. He introduced himself to Christopher and said, "Well, you have a mass. You have a lump. It's really big, and it's not benign. You've probably had it about a year."

Dr. Peters continued, stating that on Monday he would perform surgery to remove what he believed was a hyper-nephroma, a malignant tumor of the kidney. He wanted Chris to remain in the hospital until the following morning, Friday. Then he would be allowed go home to rest for the weekend. But, in order to complete the pre-surgical preparations, Chris would need to return on Sunday afternoon.

I remember the look on Chris's face. It was a half smile and at the same time a look filled with shock and disappointment. Yet, he managed to ask questions, intelligent ones that asked for information. He didn't cry. He wasn't angry. He simply listened. He just accepted.

Every word Dr. Peters spoke felt like a physical punch to my stomach. When he finished talking with Chris he said, "I'm going to step out in the hall with your mom and dad. They probably have all kinds of questions that they want to ask me. We'll be back in a little bit."

To hear him speak one might have thought we were going out into the hall to discuss where he had been on his last vacation. His composure was that of a professional who had decided long ago that he could not be objective and empathic at the same time.

While I grappled with the reality that Chris had cancer and would need surgery, I remembered a passage from a book that I had read for a graduate class called, *When Someone You Love is Dying,* by Norma Upson. The author explained that patients feel helpless when they are kept in the dark as to their true condition and are not involved in the decision making process. I instantly decided that Chris had to be 100% involved. It was his body. He was having the surgery. He was the patient. We were going to keep him informed, active and involved. It was the beginning of listening to and following my intuition. So when Dr. Peters told Chris he wanted to speak to us in the hall, I said to Chris, "Whatever we find out, we will tell you."

I never regretted that decision. Throughout the ordeal of

those next fifteen months, the knowledge that we were all in it together was the one thing that made it all possible to endure. There were no secrets to keep from Chris. That would have been destructive to Chris and we would have lost his trust.

I wrote that last paragraph seventeen years ago, shortly after Chris died. At the time I believed it to be true. Now as I reread that statement, I realize there was actually one thing we did not tell Chris; it concerned the probability of surviving a hypernephroma. I don't know whether it was due to shock, fear, disbelief, or to spare Chris. Perhaps it was all of these. But even now, years later, I still believe that to the best of our ability we were honest with Chris and he was involved in all the decisions regarding his treatment and care.

We left Chris's room and Dr. Peters walked us down the hallway. I asked Dr. Peters what Chris's chances were, but I don't exactly remember the answers, because they were so horrifying and shocking that I was unable to absorb the information. I remember he said so many percent live a year, so many percent live four to five years, and the percent that lived five years was frighteningly low. I must have been holding my breath because I was suddenly light-headed and for the first time in my life, I thought I would faint. Jack and Dr. Peters helped me to a chair and I clung to Jack's hand as he continued to listen to Dr. Peters. I was beyond participating, because I was staring into a black bottomless hole, a dark abyss. At that moment, on some level, I knew that Christopher was going to die. I knew it! And everything inside of me screamed NO! The panic that moment triggered for me continued for months and months. At that moment, I started fighting the knowledge that Christopher was going to die.

Finally, after pulling myself together, we went back into Chris's room. Chris knew I had been crying. We simply hugged and I said, "I'm sorry, Chris, I'm sorry." Chris was very calm. He was frightened and in shock. The three of us held on to each other and cried. We sat for a long time without speaking. Words were of no use. Finally and reluctantly we left Chris in his hospital room, and drove back to Indiana. During that tearful ride home, the thought that kept going through my head was, "I don't want to bury my son." This was not the way it should be. We shouldn't have to bury our children. What terrible tragedy had befallen us? We had been utterly abandoned by God.

At home Maryann and Dave, who were with us for the weekend, looked at our faces and knew the news was bad. We told them the horrifying news and as we cried, we tried to piece together the events of the last few months.

We brought Chris home the next morning so that he could rest over the weekend. He was weak and in greater pain because of the tests he had undergone, and now he had to cope with emotional pain and fear over what was yet to come. This was a cross that he was going to have to bear. As much as I needed and wanted to take the emotional and physical pain away, I could not. None of us could. We could not make it better; the most we could do was to be there with him. We could not take it away and that was the hell of it.

On Saturday, Michele and John came home too. We were in this trial together! I couldn't help thinking that God had given us two wonderful additions to our family – the baby and Dave, only to take away our son. I was angry. I cried all weekend anticipating his and our trial. I cried for Chris and for our family because we had to go through this, and I cried for myself.

I stood at the kitchen window looking out at the garden and my mind filled with images of young Christopher playing out there. Memories! Chris was only four when we started building our home. It was an event that had a great impact on him. Once he and I drove the other kids to school we'd make our daily trip to the building site where Chris would stand in one spot, arms at his sides, transfixed as he watched the carpenters measure, saw, and hammer. He was fascinated and would have remained there all day if I had let him. It was the beginning of his love for carpentry, building construction, and architecture. From then on, whenever he had the opportunity to watch carpenters at work, he was at the site absorbing and learning. As he grew, he could be found either in the family room putting together model planes, ships, and rockets, or in the garage sawing and hammering. During those years if a saw or hammer went missing, we usually looked for Chris. The garage floor was often littered with pieces of a project and layered with sawdust. No matter the project, he plunged into each with total absorption and gusto.

Chris could be obstinate and demanding especially if he thought he was right or capable. He had to do things his way and work things out for himself, and that included dealing with problems. He usually kept his feelings to himself. If I tried to draw him out and find out what was troubling him, he would react with anger and a demand to be left alone. Even John, his idol, was not often sought for advice. Sometimes he kept us all at a distance. Perhaps these qualities were the other side of self reliance. But they were qualities that sometimes worked against him.

His age or lack of experience never stopped him from tackling anything. At ten he built a wooden car from a mail order kit that was big enough for him to sit in. At Wabash College he built stage scenery and helped one of his professors with a phase of the house that he was building. One year, the only thing on his Christmas list was a list of tools. In our home, he painted, built a work bench, a storage closet, put in a sprinkler system, did household repairs. Two months before he died, I asked him why he did all these things for all of us. I remember he replied, "I always wanted to make things better." That was a significant part of who Chris was and is.

Chris was a good student, didn't cause problems, and was liked by his teachers. At Marquette High he was a favorite of one of the sisters. In her seventies, she was about 4' 11", weighted less than one hundred pounds, wore an auburn hair piece, spoke with an Irish brogue, and was a formidable force with which to reckon.

One Sunday morning after Mass, I was with Chris as he drove past the high school and spotted Sister taking a walk. He quickly pulled to the curb beside her, rolled down the window, leaned across me, and shouted, "Hi Gorgeous!" I was speechless and appalled by his boldness. A moment later, Sister leaned her head in the window, and with a big smile retorted, "Hi, handsome." I think she was blushing. Apparently they were good friends and he knew that she would be pleased and flattered. That devilish and charming brashness was a side of Chris that I didn't often see. After he died, she sent us a beautiful note in which she referred to him as, "God's Best." She told us that when she wanted an answer to prayer, she often asked Chris to intercede for her - just as we do.

Chris was a good golfer having started when he was four years old. In high school he joined the golf team and was most valuable player one year. He dated a few girls, but very quickly Ann, a beautiful blond, petite, young lady became the most important person in his life. He was thoughtful, protective, and very sweet to her. To our relief and that of her parents, neither of them smoked, drank, or used drugs.

It was so difficult for Chris to leave Ann and go off to college, that he considered working for a year so that he could be with her until she graduated from high school. He reluctantly decided to enroll at Wabash College, but turned down the invitation to be on the golf team so that he could come home weekends to be with Ann. A year later, when Ann entered college, they broke up because, understandably, she didn't want to date Chris exclusively. Unfortunately, Chris was not ready for the break-up. His dreams of a future with Ann were shattered and he became unsure of himself and depressed. So much so, that unbeknownst to us, he sought help from a counselor at Wabash. It was classic: Christopher dealing with his own problems and arriving at a solution. It wasn't until he became ill that he told me he had had counseling.

He seemed to be foundering during this period. On his weekends home from Wabash he sat on the sofa quieting watching television instead of actively engaged in one of his projects. I could see the sadness in his eyes and in his lack of animation – all unlike Chris. The life seemed to have slipped out of him. He complained about Wabash; whereas before, he had spoken highly of his teachers and of the academically challenging courses. He was confused and uncertain about his future and questioned the path he was taking.

During that time he grew more reflective and introspective. It was a dark and lonely time for him, but in hind sight, necessary for his growth. He worked through it on his own terms. The Chris that emerged from that dark tunnel was stronger, more sure of himself and the direction he wanted to take. He was ready to let go of Ann, leave Wabash, and follow his bliss into building construction. It seemed a perfect fit because he was never happier than when he was working with his hands.

By the time he transferred to Purdue he had turned a corner and was happy and enthusiastic about his future. He became more outgoing, and developed a chatty, disarming manner. His intelligence, dry sense of humor, and conversational ability were most visible in a one on one conversation. Then one noticed how articulate and sensitive he was. His views on many issues were well thought out and went right to the core of an issue. I can still visualize how he looked in his blue blazer, his eyes bright, enthusiastically talking with his hands. Precious memories of the years that were filled with promise. I desperately wished I could not turn back the clock and make the frightening present disappear.

We numbly went through the weekend in a state of shock. Cancer! Chris had cancer! It was unbelievable, horrifying. Although there are three physicians in our family, it had never entered anyone's mind that his pain was due to cancer.

On Sunday, we started phoning friends to tell them about Chris and to ask for prayers for a miracle. We were hoping against hope that Chris's tumor would turn out to be a benign mass, rather than a malignant one. My friend, Terese, called members of her prayer group, the parochial grade school and high school that Chris had attended to ask them all to pray for Chris's complete recovery. That morning, prayers were said for him at all the Sunday Masses in our parish and they would continue throughout his illness. Our family and friends in Michigan City and in other cities also began praying for Chris and those prayers continued until he died. We took consolation from the knowledge that so many people were praying for him, because we believed that prayer could change outcome. Miracles were possible.

Since hearing that Chris had cancer, my heart had been beating at an incredible rate. It continued to pound and race all weekend in response to the shattering news, but I was not frightened. I was as a third person passively observing this phenomenon and casually noting the reason why people had heart attacks when they were under stress. Surely hearts could not beat at that rate for very long without serious consequence. Yet, mine continued to do so and I could not have cared less.

Chris called his fraternity brothers to tell them he would be having surgery on Monday. They had been aware all semester that he was not well. On Sunday morning Chris's roommate, Todd came to wish him well. Before he left Todd gave him a hug. I sensed the separation Chris must be feeling. He could not return to the college life he loved so much; instead he had to walk into the unknown not knowing whether his life would ever return to what it had been.

We left for the hospital with heavy hearts sensing that a phase of our lives had come to an end. We said emotion filled good byes to Maryann, John, Michele, and Dave. Chris gave little David a kiss. What little joy Chris had had during the weekend had come from holding his three month old nephew.

Chris was admitted to the university hospital and led to a wing that was new and held state of the art monitoring equipment. A steady stream of empathic, understanding personnel came in to inform him of what would be happening the next morning. They knew more than we did about what he was about to experience and what the probable outcome would be. At that moment, though, we had all the information we could possibly handle and couldn't think ahead to outcome.

Surgery would take four to six hours, and he would be in intensive care for two to three days. Chris would not need injections for pain, because before surgery the anesthesiologist would put a catheter into his vein that would allow a continuous flow of an anesthetic that would keep Chris comfortable. I was so grateful for that. Always eager to learn, he accepted an offer to visit the intensive care unit so he could familiarize himself with the place where he would most likely spend two days. It was as much to learn something new as it was to eliminate a part of the fear of the unknown into which he would enter.

Before we left the hospital at 9:00 p.m. we prayed together and I blessed him with holy water. We hugged and kissed him and told him we would be back early in the morning. There was nothing more we were able to say to each other. We had talked over the weekend; and now, still in shock and sick at heart, we quietly left his room and drove to a nearby Holiday Inn.

We didn't sleep that night and finally at 5 a.m. we got up, dressed, and returned to the hospital. Jack and I stayed with Chris until he was taken to surgery. Numbly we accompanied him to the surgical suite where we kissed him, and I made the sign of the cross on his forehead as I had done at night when the children were little.

Jack and I went upstairs to the surgical waiting suite and began our vigil. The surgical waiting lounge was thoughtfully divided into private rooms complete with sofas and telephones so that each family had a private room in which to wait. A secretary at a central desk directed calls to the patient's family, so they would know immediately when surgery was over and when the surgeon would be down to speak to them. Before joining us, Maryann and Dave went into the surgery holding area to kiss and hug Chris before he was put to sleep. Soon John joined us and the five of us sat and waited anxiously. We tried to talk, but our eyes were on the clock, silently wondering how the surgery was going and praying for a miracle.

After four hours, I sent everyone off to have some lunch. As I sat alone, the phone rang. It was Dr. Smith. He was back from vacation and apparently had heard through the hospital grapevine that Chris was in Chicago having surgery for cancer. He asked how I was feeling. I said, "Terrible." He asked if Christopher was out of surgery yet. I answered, "No, they told us it would take four to six hours."

He responded, "That's because we are looking to see if it has spread to the blood vessels." He had the audacity to use a "we" pronoun, as though he were part of the surgical team that was removing Christopher's malignancy.

I wanted to shout at him, WE? The last time I spoke to you, you sent me to the store for cranberry juice because cranberry juice was going to dissolve his non-opaque, non-existent kidney stones. How dare he! I was so stunned by his use of the word "we" implying that he was part of the solution to Chris's medical problem that I couldn't respond to his outrageous statement. When I repeated our conversation to the family, they were as appalled and angry as I. Until he called that morning we had completely forgotten about Dr. Smith's part in all of this.

Finally, we received a call that surgery was over and that Dr. Peters would soon come down to tell us about the surgery. We sat there tense and frightened as he told us, that just as he had suspected, Chris had a hypernephroma, the worst of the kidney cancers. The tumor was still encased and they were able to remove all of it. Maryann, Dave, and Jack breathed a sigh of relief, because if it was still encased it meant that the malignancy had not had a chance to spread to surrounding tissue. Unfortunately, ten days later we learned from a resident in that department that the tumor was not encased at the time of surgery. We had no idea why he told us that it was.

23 lymph nodes had been removed and sent to the lab to determine whether any of them were malignant. His spleen was removed. A rib had been removed in order to biopsy several spots on his lung that were suspected of being malignant but proved later to be benign. But he had come through the surgery and was doing fine. We could see him in the intensive care unit at 4:00 p.m. for five minutes. Somehow we got through the afternoon and made our way to the unit.

The intensive care unit at the University hospital is an incredible miracle of modern medicine. Each unit has no more than three or four patients all of whom are monitored through an unbelievable number of lights, switches, machines, monitors, and tubing. Two to three nurses in each suite do nothing but hover over the patients. Like butterflies they are in constant motion, checking, helping, rechecking, and touching; attentive, caring, knowledgeable, and professional.

We walked in and saw Christopher. The sight was gut wrenching. Lights flashed. Monitors beeped. He was lying flat with a rolled towel under his neck. He was awake; his eyes were open. Many tubes connected him to the monitoring board behind him. He was on a ventilator, around which his teeth were clenched. An oxygen mask covered his face. He had a shunt coming from his neck and nasal gastric tube in his nose. Intravenous needles were taped to both arms.

As I looked at him, I felt immediately that I was standing at the foot of a cross. I knew how Mary felt looking at Jesus. I knew her pain and at that moment I knew she felt mine. I felt connected with every mother who had to look helplessly on as her child suffered. It was a look down through the centuries, timeless, changeless. All mothers have experienced it. There is something universal about pain, about motherhood, about witnessing the suffering of one's child, about helplessly standing by, unable to make one's child better. It doesn't change with time.

Through tears and with hearts that were breaking we talked

to him. We didn't know how much he understood, but his eyes were open. We told him it was all over, and he had done well. We told him we loved him and that we would be back at 7:00 p.m., the next visiting time.

When we left we held on to each other and sobbed. The transformation in our once healthy son had been devastating to witness. But the unit nurses said Chris was doing okay, so we clung to the hope that he would recover from the ordeal of the surgery.

Maryann and Dave had to leave to pick up the baby and drive back to Milwaukee but John remained with us. We continued to hold on to one another and sob, the image of Chris before our eyes and burned into memory. John was so overcome that he could not go in to see Chris again. We told him it was okay and encouraged him to go home. Somehow, Jack and I got through the next three hours. We forced ourselves to make phone calls to Michele, our parents and sisters telling them the devastating news that it was a hypernephroma.

At seven o'clock we went in to see Chris to find that the tube coming from his mouth had been removed. He even spoke to us. He asked me to rub his aching right arm and hand that were white, puffy, and swollen to twice the size of his left arm. His right arm had been strapped to the side on which he had been lying throughout the four and a half-hour ordeal; consequently it would take a while for the circulation to fully return. I was grateful for the chance to rub his arm; happy to do anything that would bring him some relief and allow me to have contact with him.

Since we were not going to be able to see Chris any more that night, we reluctantly left and drove back to the Holiday Inn. I remember thinking I need a drink. I don't think I'd ever thought that before. But I was too tired to drink it. Back in our room we continued to make phone calls and calls started coming in to us. We slept fitfully. Images of Chris in intensive care permeated our brief sleep. My dreams had been nightmarish since the previous Thursday when we learned of Chris's malignant tumor. That night I dreamt of a large board, on which were printed rows upon rows of numbers. The ones that were most dominant were the numbers two-two. Twenty-two. The numbers symbolized Christopher's age; he was twenty-two years old. Only twenty-two! He was so young. He should have a long life of dreams, accomplishments, and fulfillment ahead of him. Instead he would have to undergo pain, uncertainty and perhaps, even give up his future. I felt a profound sadness.

Tuesday morning we waited anxiously until we would be allowed to see Chris again. At 10 a.m. we entered his intensive care room to find that the oxygen mask had been removed, the lights were no longer flashing and he was able to speak to us. All the lines that connected him to the monitoring board had been removed and all that remained were the chest tube which drained his lung and helped to re-expand it, the line in the subclavian vein that measured his blood pressure, the IV in his arm, a catheter which drained his bladder, and a line which delivered a morphine drip into the intrathecal space.

Thankfully, in spite of all the lines he looked so much better than he had the night before. Aside from the malignancy, he was a healthy young man who had great will power and determination. The nurse said he was recovering quickly; therefore he would be able to leave the intensive care unit that day and return to his private room. We had our son back and he was healing now that the malignancy was out of his body – or so we thought.

Back in his room, Chris continued to do his best to cooperate with the nurses who provided fantastic care. Jack and I would arrive at 8 a.m. and stay until 8 p.m. We provided moral support, but because the nurses were so attentive, there was little else we could do for him except to keep him company. He did not complain of pain because the line providing morphine drip kept the pain at a minimum. Because of the surgery to his lung he had to practice taking deep breaths. He had to blow into a clear plastic hollow device that held three little balls. The harder he blew the higher the balls would go. The exercise was very

difficult for him. The first few days he could not get the balls to
rise. The exercise exhausted and frustrated him because he was
so anxious to get well and get on with his life. He was clearly
upset as he told me he couldn't do what they were asking and
fearful that this would impede his recovery. I assured him that
he was doing well, they were simply encouraging him to do a little bit more. That seemed to encourage him to keep trying. And
within a couple of days he was able to keep the balls in the air.

It was very difficult for me to accept the knowledge that my
son had cancer. It was even harder not to worry about what was
going to happen. My heart was still racing, but not constantly
as it had before. It would pound as I started thinking about
the future. The best I could do was to cope with each moment
without too much thinking. I couldn't read because I couldn't
concentrate on the words. I had no desire to write in my journal
because at that moment I couldn't write about reality. The shock
of the last few days – discovering Chris had cancer, the images of
him in intensive care, the fear of the future had put me into
overload and now I simply functioned without thinking.

Later in the week, Chris was allowed to walk and Jack and I
took turns helping Chris to walk down the hall. Jack had become
a very loving, compassionate, patient father. It was heartwarming
to observe them together. Since Chris and John had inherited
Jack's love of sports they had often exchanged sports stories.
Now Jack kept him up to date on the world of sports, read parts
of the paper to him and told him amusing anecdotes.

Toward the middle of the week, Chris wanted to shave, so
Jack shaved him. He put a hot towel on his face, lathered and
shaved him, lovingly, carefully, gently. I think that just as rub-
bing Chris's arm and doing the little things that Chris asked me
to do for him helped me, so too being able to perform this little
service for Chris was a gift to Jack as much as it was a service
for Chris.

Later in the week, Christopher, who was so fastidious, had an
accident in bed and was very embarrassed. Before he could call

for a nurse, Jack offered to help him. He became Chris's aide as he cleaned him; replaced the sheets, then asked the nurse to take the soiled sheets away. The nurse was taken aback that a father, a doctor would do something that was always left for the nurse to do.

The pain and anxiety of the previous weeks had drawn us closer and we were becoming a close knit threesome. Chris's recovery and well being were our only concern; we were not vocalizing our fears, but Jack and I did a lot of silent worrying.

John came almost every day after work. He would sit next to his brother and visit or simply watch television together much as they had done for so many years in our family room. Later in the week Maryann drove in from Milwaukee and spent the morning with Chris. And then a week after Chris's surgery, Michele came to see him. She had been keeping in contact with Chris and with us by phone but she had not seen him. Michele had always been very sensitive. She had always been very tender and kind toward Chris and since childhood they had had an empathic relationship. We understood that she had not come earlier because she could not bear to see her little brother suffering. By the time she did see him, he was a lot better but still she was shocked at his appearance. Later when she and I went for a cup of soup, she sobbed and said, "Oh, Mom, his eyes, his eyes."

I knew what she meant. Chris's eyes had always been very expressive, full of life, energy and excitement. His eyes were still expressive. But they were no longer bright and sparkling. Now what she saw expressed in them was sadness, fear, and the reality of his condition. She read it all in his eyes. Afterward she cried and grieved for several days as she remembered how he looked.

Throughout the first week that Chris was in the hospital, we had been waiting for the pathology and surgical reports. We knew that Dr. Peters had left for vacation immediately after Chris's surgery; in fact he had delayed leaving so that he could perform the surgery. However, his associate, Dr. Williams made rounds once a day accompanied by the residents and interns.

Each day we were told that the reports were not yet available.

One day when Dr. Williams, the residents and interns came in, I really looked at their faces. Dr. William's voice was cheerful but his smile was fixed. I watched the residents' faces and what I read on them turned my knees to jelly. I saw on their faces that they were writing Chris off; his cancer was so bad that there was no hope for him. When one of the residents looked at me and realized that I had been staring at him, he averted his eyes. He couldn't look in my eyes because he didn't want me to read his thoughts. I also noticed how very, very quiet they were when they walked into his room as though they dreaded walking in. As I observed their demeanor and watched their faces and their quiet manner, I sensed they were sad. I was watching them day after day. If they thought he had a good chance to recover, they would have been smiling and feeling at ease, even kidding him. They wouldn't look sad day after day. There was no need for words; their body language said it all. I tried to suppress what I had learned and hoped that I was wrong, but the following months proved that I had, indeed read the situation correctly.

The fact that nobody was giving us any reports was of great concern to all of us. This was a university hospital; how long did it take to get out a complete report? We knew it was a hypernephroma, but we did not know if malignancy had been found in the lymph nodes, and whether it had spread to the surrounding tissue and structures. It should not take a week to obtain a pathology report. Obviously, Dr. Williams was reluctant to give us the results. Later, I spoke to one of Chris's nurses about my impression. She said very honestly, that I was probably correct, because when the patient has done well and the results look good, the physician is very eager to tell the patient and the family that everything has turned out well and that the patient will have a full recovery. They do their best to assure everyone very quickly. She added that if they are dragging their feet, it is because they want the patient to recover before they say anything. Another bad sign. Another knot in my stomach. More knowledge to fight and suppress.

In the meantime, Chris was eating well and he was being praised for his swift recovery. Ten days after surgery, Chris was discharged from the hospital. As we were leaving, the nurses came in to say goodbye. The sad look on their faces told me a great deal. One of the older nurses suggested that we take along the egg crate foam pad that had been on top of Chris's mattress. Chris said no, but the nurse looked at me and urged me to take it and so we did.

The verbal and nonverbal statements that the nurses and physicians were making caused me to fear that Chris was not going to make it. It was too late. Carrying that knowledge was excruciating and every time I looked at Chris I experienced gripping fear that he would not survive this disease. Every time that thought crept into my consciousness, I rejected it and refused to accept that possibility for Christopher. Chris would not die and I would not lose him, because I was going to move heaven and earth to keep him alive. I reminded myself that we had three physicians in the family all of whom had contacts with university centers where the latest cutting edge interventions were being used. No! Chris would not die! We would not let him!

Before we left the hospital and without Chris or me knowing, Jack sought out one of the senior urology residents that had been coming in to see Chris each day and who had assisted with Chris's surgery. He asked him point blank what they had found when they did the surgery. The resident told him that the tumor had been attached to the surrounding structures. It had even grown into the renal vein and into the vena cava. They had to remove the spleen and the tail of the pancreas because the tumor had been stuck to these organs. It was totally contrary to what we had been told by Dr. Peters immediately after surgery when he informed us that the tumor had been encapsulated, meaning it had not spread to the surrounding tissue. Devastating and shocking news.

Had Doctor Peters tried to spare us until we all had had a chance to recover from the trauma of surgery? Would we have been less able to deal with truth on the day of surgery? We will never know. Later, we felt anger that Dr. Peters had not told us the truth that day. But the underlying truth is that we were angry because Chris had a tumor at all; and if he had to have one, couldn't it have been a benign tumor?

Jack did not tell anyone what had been revealed to him until he himself was able to cope with the devastating truth. But, there again we didn't tell Chris. Jack told me but either I wouldn't or couldn't work through to the conclusion that we would lose Chris. My heart and mind had rejected death as a possibility for Chris. He was going to be cured. He was going to live. I would accept nothing else.

3

HOPE AND FEAR

All of us were relieved to be home again. We arranged sofas and pillows to make Chris comfortable and placed the egg crate on his bed. He would have to limit his activity until he was fully recovered; consequently by the time he could return to school half of the semester would be over. Chris decided that he could use a break from school and would simply enjoy taking it easy, and having some fun. We heartily agreed with him. Anything, anything to make him healthy and happy again!

He had a good appetite and I indulged him. I made his favorite foods: veal scallopini, fettuccine alfredo, quiche, milk shakes. I brought home a quarter-pounder when he had a taste for one. He wanted to regain quickly the fifteen pounds that he had lost while he had been hospitalized. I wish I had known then what I learned later that summer, that cancer thrives on fat. According to macrobiotic theory when one eats foods with a high fat content the cancer is also being fed and thus, encouraged to grow. I learned this several months later when we tried the macrobiotic regimen; then later Chris's oncologist confirmed it.

Chris was quiet and somewhat withdrawn which was understandable after his hospital ordeal. But he did not complain of pain, which was surprising because of the length of his incision: from the front of his left side around the left side and to the middle of his back. But I knew he could live with a scar, no matter how long and ghastly. What mattered was that he recovered.

He received many phone calls and cards from friends. Our extended families continued to call, but Chris didn't want visitors until he felt better. He was a private person and he did not want to be seen looking frail and sickly, or to have to appear bright and cheerful when he was not feeling that way. We did not push him, because we didn't want to cause him stress, and we felt it was his right to decide when he was ready to have visitors.

After two weeks of being confined to the house, Chris complained of cabin fever. One day, he asked me to take him for a drive. I was reluctant because he had been told he had to stay at home for three weeks, but Chris persuaded me that the fresh air would be good for him. As I drove he talked about wanting to get back to his former life. He said, "Mom, I just want to get back to school, to my friends at the fraternity. It's where I want to be. I'm living for that. I've had cancer but it's over now. I just want to get on with my life."

He didn't mind the pain and the ordeal he had been through, but he did mind being away from the life he loved. He spoke of cancer in the past tense with a very positive attitude. He had such strength and focus for a young man. I was just beginning to learn what kind of man this son of ours was. I was to learn much more during the next year.

During those weeks that Chris was recovering at home, he, Jack and I and the other children spoke at length about the events leading up to the discovery of his cancer. We were appalled by our blindness and by the knowledge that we had placed our total faith in a specialist and friend in whose competency we now had serious misgivings. We were terrified to think about the irreparable harm the three and a half month delay would have on Chris's chances. We berated ourselves for not having taken Chris to another urologist back in October when Dr. Smith could not determine the cause of the pain. Jack, Maryann, and Dave felt terrible guilt for not having seen what was now obvious.

Jack wondered whether there was any indication on the x-ray of last October that Chris had cancer. One day at the office, he looked in Chris's medical file and sought out the retrograde renal x-ray report from October that had been taken at the hospital in Michigan City. He was stunned by what he read. The report said that there was no verifiable diagnosis, but Chris should have follow up studies done, including an ultrasound as soon as possible. It was now obvious that Dr. Smith had not read the report from the radiologist or he would have had those studies done while Chris was still in the hospital when he was first treated in October. Jack was shocked not only with Dr. Smith's mistake but also by the lack of responsibility shown by the radiologist, who should have asked Dr. Smith why his patient had not come in for further studies. It seemed that everyone had messed up.

Now, all we could do was to make sure that Chris had the best care available. Chris's own attitude was very positive. He felt that the ordeal was over, the cancer was removed, and he was ready to resume his life. We knew his positive attitude was important to his recovery. No matter what our fears were, we wanted him to be positive toward his recovery and his future. No matter what we were told as to his chances, we knew that Chris was going to fully recover because God would not let us down. We were praying very hard and we knew that many people from all faiths had been praying for Chris since learning of his surgery.

Looking back I perceive my prayers as frantic and desperate, as I tried to suppress the terror that came up whenever I thought that Chris could die. I was praying to God the Father to whom I rarely prayed for help. As a Catholic girl and woman, I had always sought out the Blessed Mother. But subconsciously I must have realized that in matters of life and death, I needed God to listen to my plea, because only He could answer my prayer.

The third week after Chris's surgery we went in to see Dr. Peters. We already had been given the report by phone that one lymph node out of the twenty three that had been removed had been positive for cancer, meaning that Chris was now considered to be at stage two. Dr. Peters stepped into the waiting room and asked if Jack and I wished to speak to him without Chris being present. We said no, we would speak to him together. Were we afraid to hear what he would tell us if Chris were not present? Did we not want Chris to feel that he was out of the loop of information? Were we challenging him to tell all of us the truth? I believe it must have been a combination of all of these because Jack and I said no at the same time. Yet we had kept from Chris the information that the resident had given Jack. Looking back, I believe that if we had spoken to him without Chris's presence he would have told us that the cancer was more advanced than he had indicated on the day of surgery. What is more to the point is that he told Chris he did not need radiation or chemotherapy and he could return to school. Had he written Chris off? If he was at a more advanced stage of cancer, shouldn't he have told Chris he needed to begin chemotherapy and or radiation therapy at once?

In retrospect I can think of many should haves. Jack should have told him what the resident had said. We should have asked him about chemotherapy and radiation. Jack, as a physician should have had many questions. But the truth was that in that office that day Jack was not a physician, he was a parent, a scared parent just as I was. And when Dr. Peters said Chris did not need therapy we, like Chris breathed a sigh of relief. We wanted to believe that this excellent surgeon knew what was best for Chris.

As we were leaving, Dr. Peters said, "I didn't get a phone call from Dr. Smith. Tell him not to be too embarrassed." He was referring to the fact that as Chris's physician, Dr. Smith would have been expected to call Dr. Peters to receive a medical report as to Chris's progress and prognosis. As Dr. Smith did not call, Dr. Peters assumed that having misdiagnosed Chris, he was too embarrassed to call. I said nothing, but I thought Dr. Smith should be mortified by his mismanagement of Chris's case.

We drove home from Chicago on a rather happy note. We wanted to believe that Chris not needing chemotherapy or radiation were good signs not bad. Chris was elated. I remember he was wearing a navy blazer with an argyle sweater and a powder blue shirt and he looked handsome and healthy. Dr. Peters had given him permission to drive; and as soon as we arrived Chris left for Purdue for an overnight visit with friends. I had suggested that he wait a few more days before making the two hour drive but he said, "Mom, please don't stop me. It's where I want to be. I want to be with my friends back at school. This is what I'm living for." We were relieved and happy that he was resuming his old life. For a brief moment we felt that things could return to normal again.

He came back from Purdue refreshed and happy, and made the trip three more times during March and early April. Jack and I had been planning a trip to Florida in May and we encouraged Chris to come along. After some deliberation he decided he would like to join us.

Then one Monday morning in April, after a weekend at Purdue, he walked into the family room, stretched out on the couch, and said he had been having terrible back pain. He had gone to a Sorority Spring Formal dance where he had tripped and fallen. He thought that perhaps the pain in his back was due to the fall or to the strain of driving back and forth from Purdue. Even though he had been using Jack's car which had an automatic shift, driving still seemed to cause strain to his back. At least we hoped that was the cause.

However the pain continued and we returned to Dr. Peters who said he wanted Chris to have a bone scan, chest x-ray, and acid phosphatase test within the next two weeks. On learning that we were planning a trip to Florida, he said the tests could wait until Chris returned.

❧ 4 ❧

FLORIDA – RENEWAL AND REALITY

The night before we flew to Florida, we stayed in a hotel near the airport and had dinner at a favorite Italian restaurant. Christopher was cheerful and happy. We were in a party mood and looked forward to our vacation. Emotionally and physically we had felt the strain of the last three months. We shared a bottle of wine and ordered much too much food for the three of us. The aroma of our favorite Italian specialties combined with the pleasant atmosphere and the joy of being together were having their usual affect on us. We laughed and joked through dinner. When the waitress discovered I too was Italian, it became ethnic night. She and I told Jack and Chris stories about "funny" relatives and old superstitions and customs. She and I had many happy memories of St. Joseph Tables held on March 19th each year. Chris told us that his least favorite great-aunt was the one who pinched his cheek every time she saw him. Our waitress said, "Honey, every Italian family has one of those!" We had Chris doubled over with laughter. It was a very beautiful evening and one that we still remember with tenderness.

By the time we arrived at the condo, Chris was in love with Long Boat Key and St. Armand Circle. Although we had been there several times, this was Chris's first trip. Now, he walked around the condo approvingly. It had been newly decorated and the place was fresh and attractive. As he looked out at the Gulf of Mexico he sounded like his usual enthusiastic self.

Because of his background in building construction and his love of architecture, he enjoyed our drives on Long Boat, Anna Maria, and Casey keys. We spent one day looking at new model condominiums. Chris was in seventh heaven. He was his old self – full of information, talkative, enthusiastic, absorbing knowledge. It had always been Chris's way to pace back and forth with his hands in his pockets whenever he became excited. Now as he paced back and forth and spoke excitedly, I realized how much I had missed this Chris, the happy Chris.

Jack and I delighted in taking him to all of our favorite places like the little French bakery and pastry shop on St. Armand's Circle. One afternoon after shopping, we went there for lunch. Chris loved it. He thought we should order six desserts because he wanted to taste everything. So we did and gorged on sweets.

On some level, without having to verbalize it, we were indulging each other and ourselves, trying to fill this time with beautiful and funny memories that would have to last a lifetime; because the pain that started two weeks before had not subsided. By the time we arrived in Florida, Chris was taking pain pills regularly. Mornings were the worst. He would wake up with acute pain, take a pain pill, then move to the sofa and wait for the pill to take effect. We prayed that the pain was due to an acutely strained muscle that improved once Chris was up and about. But when the pain continued day after day, inwardly our spirits sank. But in spite of the fact that Chris was fighting pain most of the time, he did his best to enjoy each day.

He loved St. Armand's Circle. It is always alive with vacationers many of whom come from Canada and Europe. The circle is shaped like the spokes of a wheel with interesting shops and restaurants and a park in the center of the circle. Chris loved walking around the circle, but he could only walk around part of it before the pain would increase and we would have to return to the car.

We took Chris to all the places that had become our favorites during the years that we had been coming to the Key. We took him to a Crab House, an unpretentious restaurant on the bay with a view of Sarasota. As we ate hush puppies and boiled shrimp in a basket; we watched boaters and fishermen tie up their boats and come in for lunch. Later we strolled out to the docks to see whether we could catch a glimpse of the dolphin that made its home in the adjacent waters. Chris loved these restaurants which were so different from the typical midwestern ones. We loved to watch him forget his discomfort and enjoy himself for little while. How we regretted never having taken the time to do this before he became ill.

One evening we went to an Italian restaurant in Sarasota. We stuffed ourselves on the little dinner rolls that came clustered together and rolled in olive oil, basil and garlic. He drank wine, and we drank wine. We had a splendid time. I kidded Chris about the fact that I had never worried that he would ever want to use drugs to get high, because he liked garlic so much that he would rather get high on garlic. I remember that statement with sadness, because ironically within a few short months he was put on morphine to relieve the pain, and he would be on a steadily increasing dose until his death.

Another important part of our experience was attending St. Mary Star of the Sea Catholic Church that had become our parish away from home. The floor to ceiling mural behind the altar, painted by a local artist, depicted Jesus on a sandy beach surrounded by people with the Sea of Galilee in the background. He has a gentle smile on his face and eyes that look tired but compassionate and kind. With his hands before him, he holds two pieces of bread. Looking at it, one feels that Jesus is offering us not only the bread but also himself. It's an inspiring and beautiful portrayal of Jesus. A year later, it was this image of Jesus that we wanted to have carved on Chris's headstone. Unfortunately, we did not have permission or a picture to show the stone carver. We settled for another image, one of the resurrected Jesus that we liked almost as well.

We loved our time together. But there was urgency about it. It was our time not to think about the future and what Chris's pain meant. But we knew we would soon have to return and address the problems. I wondered if we would ever have another vacation together. We did not.

Chris had a bone scan soon after we returned and the results were sent to the University hospital in Chicago. After what seemed like an endless wait, we received word of the result. Chris had gone to the Mall on a quick errand. Jack was to receive the call at his office. I nervously waited at home for a call from Jack. When I finally called him, I learned he was on his way home. I knew immediately that the news was bad, because Jack wanted to be with us when he told us.

I walked out of the house as he drove up; I saw the strained look on his face and knew that Christopher had metastases. I fell apart. I cried hysterically, wanting to push back the horrible truth, feeling helpless, knowing that his pain would be increasing. I was afraid to know any more than I already knew. When Chris returned he read our faces and knew that the cancer had spread to his spine. Helplessly we hugged one another and cried.

Finally, we called the children and broke the devastating news to them. It was hard on them too, because they wanted to be with us during this terrible time. But since they all lived and worked in other cities, the best we could do was keep everyone informed by phone.

Now we knew for sure what had been causing Chris's back pain. The kidney cell cancer had spread to his spine. Surgery had not "gotten all of it." Now what? Chemotherapy? What kind? What would give him the best chance to recover? Jack said Dr. Peters wanted Chris to begin Interferon chemotherapy at the University hospital. Was that the best course to take? We knew we had to have more information before we could make a good decision. Maryann and Dave encouraged us to meet with the head of oncology at the Medical Center where they were receiving their medical training. Dr. Paul (fictitious name) had trained at the National Cancer Institute in Washington D.C. Surely, he would be able to give us another opinion on the course that Chris should take. We made an appointment to see him on May 23rd. Our spirits lifted a little.

The day before the appointment we drove to Maryann and David's house in Milwaukee. That evening the six of us went out to dinner. We were thinking positively and our spirits were up as we purposely told funny stories so that we would laugh. Six-month-old David amused us as he tried to sip water from a glass – a new experience. Chris told a story about Jack that took place when we were in Florida. Again, without verbalizing it, we realized how precious these times were, and we did the best we could to create lasting memories of happy times.

The next day the five of us went to the oncology floor of the medical college to meet with the oncologist, Dr. Paul. It was dreary. The rooms were small and dark. As we walked through we saw people in the halls receiving chemo treatments through IVs. Emaciated people walked down the hall holding on to walkers. Many people were in beds. But they were all old people. They had gray hair. At least those were the only ones I remember. My son was 22, and looked healthy now that he had regained the weight. He did not belong in this ward with all these old sick people.

Chris had several blood tests, and then we met with Dr. Paul. He was very kind, spoke to us at great length and after asking Christopher about his surgery, he spoke about options and alternatives. Chris's best chance would be to get accepted into National Cancer Institute's new and still experimental Interleukin II program. He quoted statistics that indicated Interleukin II had a better response rate than other chemotherapies. Chris asked him a number of questions, and satisfied with the answers; he said he wanted to try to get into the program instead of going on Interferon – the chemo that had been suggested by Dr. Peters at the university hospital in Chicago.

Dr. Paul told Jack to write a letter to Dr. Rosenberg indicating that Chris wished to be considered as a candidate for the Interleukin II program. He also told us to write to the other six National Cancer Institute centers that were located in other parts of the country that also were using Interleukin II. In that way, if the Washington D.C. center could not take him, he would be able to have the chemotherapy at one of the other centers. When the letters were written, he would add a personal note to each recommending that Chris be accepted to the protocol. He personally knew Dr. Rosenberg and many of the physicians who ran the programs at the other centers. He said that Christopher had an excellent chance of getting into the Interleukin II program, because he was young and healthy, and because Interleukin research was being done on renal cell cancer, the type of kidney cell cancer that Chris had. So he was an excellent candidate. Thanks be to God.

Dr. Paul suggested that while Chris waited to be accepted at National Cancer Institute that he have a course of radiation to deter the cancer from spreading any further. Radiation therapy would not prevent Chris from being eligible for the Interleukin protocol. However, he cautioned that Chris could not have any other kind of chemotherapy while he waited to be accepted, because the results would then be clouded. In other words if Chris showed improvement it could not be proven that the cause was due to Interleukin II and not from another chemotherapy.

Hearing this, I knew that Chris was committing to being accepted at NCI. What if he was not accepted? Would it be too late to do anything else? I pushed the thought away. I was in a room with four physicians, one of whom was head of oncology and knew far more than all the rest of us about cancer and what worked and what did not; and he was telling us that this was the best course of action for Christopher. So I tried to banish my fear but it was always there, emerging as troubled, nightmarish dreams.

On the whole, we came away from the meeting feeling encouraged that there was a therapy that would cure Chris. He was making the right choice. We knew Chris would be accepted for this new chemotherapy, and he would get well, because he was strong, determined, and motivated. Surely the saints to whom we had been praying would intercede and ask God to grant us this request. He just had to.

We left Milwaukee and drove directly to the University hospital in Chicago where we had an appointment with Dr. Peters. Chris explained to him that he knew that there was only a 10% chance that kidney cell cancer would respond to Interferon chemotherapy. Therefore he had decided to apply for the Interleukin II protocol, but he would like to start radiation therapy at the university center right away. Doctor Peters agreed that Chris was making a good decision, and arranged for Chris to have the first treatment of radiation immediately.

We entered the radiation oncology department to discover that Carrie, one of the nurses that had taken care of Chris when he had his surgery, was now working in radiation oncology. They were about the same age and her friendly and familiar face was a welcome sight for Chris. She took us through the department, gave us information and booklets; and then gave Chris his first treatment of radiation. Chris was not frightened or intimidated by the treatment. In fact the machinery fascinated him.

Chris read the books Carrie gave him, and learned that he might be nauseated by the treatment; therefore fatty, greasy foods should be avoided. Since he would be thirsty after the treatments, we would bring bottled water with us each day when we came into Chicago. He would receive radiation five days a week for several weeks, the proposed length of the course of treatment.

Chris began radiation therapy, and I dropped out of the Masters Program. In February, when Chris was diagnosed with cancer and was to have surgery, I had said, "Chris, I'll be here for you until you're well and don't need me anymore." I was trying to reassure him and myself that he was going to get well, and in the mean time he would not be doing it alone.

Chris had smiled and said, "Thanks, Mom."

After he came home from the hospital, I managed the one evening a week class. However, I was too distracted by my concern for Chris to study and complete course requirements.

My professors kindly gave me an extension of one year to complete the requirements. But when Chris needed radiation treatments, my degree and my plans paled before my desire to be with him during this catastrophic time. So when I made the decision to drop out of school, it was amazingly simple.

For the next four weeks Chris had radiation Monday through Friday. Our early morning drives through rush hour traffic on the Dan Ryan expressway were very quiet and sad. I tried to keep my fearful thoughts at bay because I couldn't lose control. I had to stay focused on my driving and get Chris through this ordeal. But inside I was in shock and disbelief over what I was doing. I was actually taking my son for radiation treatment for cancer. This reality was so horrible that I had to keep shutting down my mind in order to function. At the hospital Chris was treated quickly and kindly for which we were both grateful. Although I sat in the waiting room, a part of me was inside with Chris praying that the radiation was zapping the malignancy and destroying it.

Chris was tolerating radiation fairly well. Sips of water and crackers helped to reduce the nausea and thirst, and by dinner, he was able to eat a small meal.

The second week of June, Chris thought he felt a different kind of pain. He had more tests and while we waited anxiously for the results he continued with radiation. On June 12, Jack drove Chris to Chicago for Chris's treatment and returned quickly, because Chris did not have radiation that day. Treatment had been discontinued. The test results had shown metastases to the liver. It was another black day in our lives. Learning that he had metastases to the liver was a catastrophe that shattered Chris and our family. Would the horrible news never end? In anger and frustration, Jack expressed what we were all feeling. "When is Chris going to catch a break? When are we going to start getting some good news?"

From the beginning Chris had accepted his circumstances without bitterness or anger. He went through surgery with a good attitude, recovered very quickly, and did not complain about the pain or the surgical ordeal. He simply did what he had to in order to recover quickly, because what was of paramount importance to him was that he return to college as soon as possible. He was looking forward to the Fall semester with great anticipation, because then he could resume his real life.

He was shattered when he learned that the cancer had metastasized and he would not be returning to school in the Fall. If he hadn't been in so much pain, he would have moved heaven and earth to do so. Instead he would have to apply for and hope that he would be accepted for Interleukin chemotherapy. As was his way, he quietly, thoughtfully meditated on his circumstances, asked questions of his doctors, his siblings, of Jack and me, and after quiet deliberation and I believe a strong infusion of grace, he resigned himself to this new condition and moved on to the next step.

As devastated as we were, we couldn't afford the luxury of giving in to our growing depression. There was no time to fall apart. We tried to be strong because we needed to support Chris. And if Chris was to survive this nightmare, we had to focus on getting him into the Interleukin II protocol. When we had met with Dr. Paul he had told us that National Cancer Institute would not accept Chris for the Interleukin II program unless or until he had metastases to soft tissue. Consequently, we had held off writing to them, because the earlier tests indicated that he did not have metastasis to soft tissue. Now the letters were composed and sent to Dr. Paul. He attached a note to each letter and sent them on to Washington D.C., Frederick, Maryland, and to the other centers around the country. We waited with great anxiety for two weeks, and then we heard from NCI in Washington. Dr. Rosenburg's resident called and asked for all of Christopher's files. Praise the Lord! It was good news! Chris had a chance. We dared to rejoice. Chris called his brother and sisters to share the good news with them. We immediately obtained his file and sent it to NCI. And then we waited.

Chris talked with Maryann or Dave, and John and Michele almost every day. We were all in this together; this was an aspect of medicine that was new to all of us. Should we be doing something while we waited? How long would it take to hear from them? We had lots of questions but no answers. Finally, with input from Maryann and Dave, Chris decided to get a second opinion and keep a long-standing appointment with the head of oncology at the University hospital in Chicago.

The doctor thought that Chris was there to begin chemotherapy that day. But Chris said no, explaining that he wanted to get into the Interleukin II program. The physician was not encouraging, because he said everyone was trying to get into that program. However, when he learned that this was Chris's decision, he said he would do all that he could to help us. He also confirmed that the Interferon that he was prepared to give to Chris had a less than ten per-cent response rate. A response rate, not a cure rate. It seemed as though we were doing the right thing by turning down Interferon and waiting for Interleukin II through NCI.

WAITING AND AWAKENING

That long summer while we waited anxiously for word from NCI, our entire family was invited to my Sister Joanne's home. It was good to be with family members who knew what we were going through, and a welcomed break from the tension and anxiety of waiting to hear from NCI. But it was also hard to participate in this gathering of family because it sharply pointed out how different our lives had become.

Jack, Chris, and I were quiet on the long trip home, each of us caught up in our own thoughts, yet each of us thinking the same thoughts – always about Chris. When we returned Chris went directly up to his room. After a few minutes I followed and asked him if he wanted company. He was lying across his bed. I sat down next to him. His eyes were red from crying. He said, "For the first time since all this started, I am angry that I have cancer. Being with all of the family today was good, but it was so hard. I don't want to go through this anymore. I want it to be over. I just want to be able to have a normal life. I want to be with my family and just be like everyone else."

I believe until then he had been in denial. Now it was dawning on him that there was a huge gulf separating him from the rest of the family and from his friends. He alone was going through a physical, emotional, and spiritual trial from which he would not emerge the same, and it separated him from everyone else.

We were both crying. On a soul level I was there with him feeling how he felt. It was happening to both of us. But the torture for me was that I couldn't release him from cancer, from his physical and emotional pain and take it all on myself. I would have given anything to take his place and free him to live his dreams. But I couldn't give him that gift. The only recourse I had was to give him some hope, some insight that would make his trial easier.

We talked about death, and I related a realization that I had about life. I told him that, "Each life in the light of eternity is but a blink of an eye. All of us living right now are here for just a brief moment in time; even if we live to be one hundred we can still count our lives in number of days. Our real home is in the next life and even if one of us goes before the others, very soon we will all be there together."

Christopher listened and he understood. He would benefit from more spiritual guidance than I could give him, so I asked if he would like to talk to Father Bertino, his friend and former high school teacher and golf coach who had since been transferred to a high school thirty miles away. He said, "Yes, I'll call him. But I'm not sure he even knows that I've had cancer. Now I have to tell him that it has metastasized. I'm afraid it will be a shock for him."

The following week, he did go to see Bert, as Chris called him. They had gone for pizza and then had taken a ride. On their return to the rectory, they sat on Father's veranda, and he broke the news that he had metastatic cancer. They talked for a long while, and then went back to Father's apartment where he gave Chris the Sacrament of the Sick. When he turned home, he said, "I feel at peace now that I have talked with Bert and he gave me the Sacrament of the Sick. Whatever happens now will be okay. I'm at peace with everything."

And he was peaceful. I believe the grace he received from the Sacrament gave him the strength to accept and endure the emotionally and physically painful months that were to come.

During that most difficult summer of 1986 very few events were pleasant, but there was an occasion that stands out in my memory. On the Fourth of July John, Chris, Jack and I were invited to a back yard barbecue with several families of close friends.

Our children had been in grade school and high school together. Now they were either in college or recently graduated, working and living away from home. This was an opportunity for them to visit and catch up.

Our friends and our small community were aware that Chris had had surgery for cancer; and he had to field difficult questions about his health whenever he left the house. I am sure that day he was asked how he was feeling and I am also sure that Chris responded with "great" because he wanted to fit in among his peers - to be just like everyone else. I observed this group of magnificent young adults. I imagined them embarking on their life careers, marrying, starting families. I fervently prayed that those dreams would be for Chris too.

After lunch there was a rousing game of volleyball. Chris was out there hitting the ball just like everyone else. Jack and I would look at each other and wince every time he hit the ball. We wondered how much pain he was enduring in order to be part of the group. We knew that more than anything, for today, it was important for him to feel like everyone else, to fit in.

After the barbecue, he was invited to watch the fireworks display. So he drove off in his Honda and continued the celebration of the Fourth of July, his favorite holiday.

Earlier in the spring, Chris told me that he had so many plans for his future and had always lived for the future. He said he lived twenty per cent in the present and eighty per cent in the future. I suggested that he live fully in the present because the present is all that any of us really have. After that, I noticed that he took every opportunity that presented itself. However, I worried about how much "present" he had left.

More and more incapacitated by pain, he had to keep increasing the amount and the strength of the pills he was taking for pain. But he tried to hold on to his life as he wanted it to be. So, in spite of the pain, he made as many trips as he could to Purdue to be with his fraternity and sorority friends and they came to visit him. He was still able to drive; a blessing that gave him freedom and mobility, gifts that he was to grieve the loss of later on. In the evening he'd drive to the lake to photograph or to simply watch his beloved sunsets, or visit with friends.

Although he had to limit his physical activity, he managed to keep busy with one of his many interests. I remember a tape that Chris made that last summer. Chris had gone out after dinner but returned earlier than usual and went up to his room. A storm was brewing. He placed a tape recorder with a microphone at the open window in his bedroom and recorded the storm. Then he brought it down to the family room and the three of us listened to it together. He had captured the rumbling of distant thunder and of rain falling softly on the leaves. And then the loud explosions of sound as the storm moved overhead bringing torrential rain that pounded on the courtyard brick. The wind increased in momentum and we heard it blow against the screen of the open window making a whistling sound. I remember we were feeling sad and depressed that night and the storm captured and reflected our mood. It was as though even the heavens were mourning with us. We had probably had another setback. I don't remember, as there were so many. So much waiting. So much worry. So much anxiety.

In spite of the horrendous news that he had metastatic cancer and would not be returning to school, he nevertheless wanted to be productive and to engage in some project that would be worthwhile. So after careful thought he decided to offer his help to Marquette High School, his alma mater. The editor of the school paper was a young man he knew and whose Sister Chris had dated. He said that offering to assist Colby with the paper would be worthwhile for both himself and for Marquette.

For this project Chris needed a better computer and printer. One day, he happily came back with his trunk loaded with a new computer and printer. In a state of excitement, just like the old Chris, he explained that learning to use the new computer would be his project for the Fall while he was on the Interleukin II protocol.

During the early summer he spent many hours at the computer. It was a godsend, because he was no longer able to be physically active, and it was challenging enough to hold his attention and even distract him from the ever increasing pain. As hard as it was, he managed to maintain a good quality of life filling it with people that he loved and projects that challenged him.

By the end of summer, he had less physical energy and greater back pain; consequently he was unable to sit at the computer for any length of time. The time that he was there was extremely painful for him; but still he persisted as he helped Colby with the first printing of the weekly paper. But sadly, he had to discontinue his work with Colby and the school paper because he could no longer work at the computer or even go up and down the stairs more than once a day.

As the summer dragged on, Chris spent more time in the house. He tried to store up his energy so that he could go out once a day, usually in the evening. He would drive to the lake, watch the sunset and come home. He was sadder and sadder as he realized what was happening to his body. The reality of his situation was becoming horribly apparent to us. But we clung to the hope that Interleukin was going to come through for him and cure him.

Since he had less energy for physical activity, he resumed working on models. He started putting together small rockets similar to 4th of July firecrackers. One day, he assembled all of the rockets that he had made and then within a two or three day period, he brought all of them outside to our driveway and set all of them off. I think he used them all up, because he knew that this was going to be the last time that he would have the energy to do so. Watching him was heart wrenching, because I knew that he was saying goodbye to a hobby that he had always enjoyed. But it was a symbol of more than that. He was acknowledging a death, the end of that part of his life when he had been healthy, strong, and free to do all the things that he loved.

Shortly after that, he said that he wanted to build a kite. Would I help him? The two of us set out for the fabric store, where he selected a fabric that he felt was sturdy enough and the two of us spent a few hours working together. I cut and sewed the fabric onto the frame that he made. He said, "Mom, I'm going to take it to Mt. Baldy and fly it." Unfortunately, by the time he decided to make a kite, he was in too much pain to walk up to the top of Mt. Baldy, and so the kite rested on the rec room pool table until after his death. Then I hung it on the wall of his room. Whenever I see it, it reminds me of Chris's indomitable spirit and of the sweet time we had making it together. It was a simple project, one that I would expect a much younger child to undertake. I think it was probably one of the many projects that Chris had wanted to do in his life-time, and one that was still possible for him to undertake now that he was so incapacitated.

Unfortunately, flying it was beyond him. But on a special day, I hope to assemble our family on top of Mt. Baldy where we will fly it and then release it as I believe Chris had intended to do. (We did fly the kite on Chris's 36th birthday – New Year's Eve – 1999. An unusually warm day. Our family gath-ered together on the beach in front of our home and watched as Chris's beloved brother, John and Dave flew Chris's kite.)

One day after we made the kite together, Chris asked me to bring down a green metal container from his room that con-tained his art supplies. Now, unable to move easily, he spent his time on the sofa, drawing and sketching. But in frustration he gave up quickly. Finally, at the end of that week, a few days before he was paralyzed, he worked on crossword puzzles. These are only a few examples of Christopher's indomitable spirit and will to live. With remarkable courage, when one door closed, he opened another.

Waiting was easier said than done. The endless summer dragged on, one long day after another without word from National Cancer Institute as to the reason for the delay in call-ing Chris to NCI in Washington or to one of the other regional Centers to begin treatment. The several phone calls we did receive from NCI were to request that Chris have more tests. During the summer we made several more trips into the University hospital in Chicago for more tests, quickly dispatching the results to NCI. And then more waiting. Finally in desperation we resorted to writing letters and making calls to NCI asking for information as to Chris's status. And then we waited and agonized and prayed.

The worse part was that while we waited to hear, Chris wasn't receiving chemotherapy or even radiation to deter the spread of malignancy. I'd wake up in the middle of the night in panic, wondering what was happening in Chris's body. What was the cancer doing? Was it growing? If so, where? To his brain? The same questions terrorized us all. I struggled through each day trying not to think negatively, praying and hoping that we would soon hear that Chris was accepted for the Interleukin II treatment that would surely save his life.

We were so worried that left unchecked the cancer was spreading, that Jack called NCI to ask them if Chris could have another series of radiation treatments since the first radiation series had been aborted. They told him to go ahead. Again we drove in five days a week for another series of radiation treatments. This time since he was receiving stronger radiation, the course would last for only seventeen days. But what NCI did not tell Jack when he had called them for permission, and what we did not learn until after he had the course of treatment, was that Chris would have to wait a month after treatment had stopped before he would be seen by NCI. In effect, our attempt to slow the cancer had in actuality slowed the process which could save Chris's life. Words cannot describe the sorrow and fear and anguish that washed over us when we heard this devastating news.

Why had we not been completely informed as to the consequences of more radiation treatment? Where had communication broken down? Were we not asking the right questions? Were we speaking to uninformed medical personnel? In the years that Jack had been in medicine we had always trusted the medical process. The faith that we had had in medicine was now badly shaken. It was no longer the bulwark upon which we could rely. This medicine had new words, new rules, or no rules that were reliable. Rather, I felt that we had been flung way out into outer space where the terrain was new and unexplored and the way unclear. We had been forced to learn a new medical language, and then wait interminably while a chain of command made up of unknown physicians with unfamiliar names and faces made medical decisions that would determine Christopher's fate. We desperately wanted to return to the medicine that was familiar, solid, and dependable, but we didn't know how to return to earth.

Fear was always present. What if? What if he was not accepted soon enough or not accepted at all? As soon as that thought rose to consciousness, I would slam the door on it. But in unguarded moments the thought would reoccur causing me intense anguish. I read the same worry on Chris's and Jack's faces but we were too scared to speak the words.

Anxiety was my constant companion now. Perhaps as a mother I had always lived with some measure of anxiety. Some women are natural born mothers. I was not. I was too anxious. Perhaps the reason was the family system into which I was born. It was one that had survived the loss of two infants plus a couple of miscarriages. My parents lost their first child, their only son a day after his birth, and then a year before my own birth, they lost my two year old sister. This last tragedy had a great impact on me, because I was born into a sad family that was grieving the loss of a beautiful, blond, blue eyed, impish two year-old.

Throughout my childhood and into my early teens, my mother would recount the events leading up to Gen's death, and each time she told the story, I could feel her pain reach down into my heart and squeeze it until I thought my heart would break, and I would dissolve in tears. I suppose my mother's purpose in retelling the story was to relieve her own pain and to bring my sister to life for me. But I was too little and too fragile to share this pain with her, with the result that throughout my life emotional pain, mine and that of others, is the hardest aspect of life for me to endure. Perhaps it is because I started experiencing it so early in life. From childhood I knew that to lose a child was an unspeakable horror.

Because of my family history, I took the responsibility of parenting very seriously; I worked hard at it. But I was not a relaxed mother, nor particularly adept at having fun being a mother. The powerful lesson that I learned at a very early age, namely, that life is fragile and children die, impacted on the way I reared my children. And so my focus was on keeping them safe and healthy. Loving and caring for my children for the rest of my life was a commitment that was ingrained in me. I would do anything to protect them from dying and from experiencing my parents' tragedy. Unfortunately, despite my determination and commitment to protect them from harm, I too would come to experience the loss of a beloved child. Not only me. There are twenty-three of us who are first cousins. Of those, eight of us have lost a child from eight different causes. Six of them were young men in their prime. Tragically we have learned over and over again that children die.

But as the years went by, the anxieties that I had felt when the children were infants, especially with Christopher, faded away, for the most part due to experiences dealing with many situations that I felt I handled successfully. I learned not to panic when one of the children became ill, even with serious illness. I thought with gratitude that my children were safe because, as a medical family we were aware of the many medical resources from which to draw. And so I had learned to be confident both in medicine and in my ability to protect my children.

When we discovered Chris's cancer, I was knocked to my knees. It was a shock that permeated my entire being and my life imploded. It was as though a bar had been stuck into the spokes of our well ordered life. It took away my self assurance that I had a solid grasp on my life and on my world. It was devastating to know that I didn't. How could this be? My whole being wanted to disbelieve. There was some mistake. Surely surgery would prove that this mass was a benign tumor, not cancer. But surgery provided the indisputable and shattering truth, Chris had cancer. What would happen to Chris? To his plans for his future, to our plans, to the feeling of contentment with life as it was? I couldn't or wouldn't grasp this horrible, shocking reality. I could not lose my son! I could not relive my mother's fate. I desperately wanted to turn back the clock and go back to my life, to my world where my family was happy and healthy, to the way things were, to feel like me again.

All of my life I had unconsciously been building an aura, a persona that I saw as being me: my attitudes, beliefs, preferences, successes and failures, the image I had of myself. From the very beginning of Chris's illness, I started to lose parts of that persona, the person I thought I was. I felt I was being broken down then rebuilt in a different configuration, like a child's tinker toy is taken apart and reshaped to become something else.

Perhaps I was shedding parts of myself because they had become unimportant. I no longer had the time or the energy; I was too distracted to be a friend even to my closest friends. I gave up my usual activities and lunches with friends. Jack and I took Chris out for dinner once a week, but now we rarely went out with friends. Our time was spent with Chris and with our other children when they came on weekends. Jack and I spoke with our children each day to reassure ourselves that they were okay and to keep them updated. And then we focused on Chris. I no longer found it important to be a student working toward a master's degree that no longer mattered enough to pursue. It was as though a dark shade had been drawn across my eyes and I could no longer see the sun shine or experience joy. Life had become assorted shades of gray devoid of music, laughter, joy, contentment, or peace. It was now filled with anxiety, fear, and grief.

Gone were the days when I felt confident and on the right track. As I witnessed Chris's suffering and deterioration each day, I seemed to lose more of my former self. The image I have is of a brick building. I see the exterior façade slowly falling, brick by brick until what is left and exposed is only the interior.

It wasn't simply the outer aspects of my life that were affected. It went deep to the core of my personhood and spirit, and I didn't know this person whom I had become. This new me lived with terror awake or asleep. She stayed to herself. She felt empty and hollow and yet filled with emotional pain. She grieved all the time. She felt Chris's pain as acutely as her own. She couldn't seem to speak without tears slipping out of her eyes and sliding down her face. She was a displaced person who was anxiously trying to accommodate and adjust to this terrifying world in which she found herself. Her prayers were anxious as they tumbled from her lips. She found no comfort in her usual hobbies. Her mind was too preoccupied to absorb what she read. Cooking was a temporary distraction that seemed to justify itself, because it brought a measure of enjoyment to Chris, Jack, and the other children when they were present.

As Chris grew sicker, more and more of my former persona faded away as I became focused on only one thing: making Chris's life as comfortable as possible. I had only one role. Chris's mother. Now my life revolved around his needs.

Our family offered Chris what support we were able to give. Except for taking care of his practice, Jack too, had withdrawn from all of his outside activities including his position as trustee of the Indiana Medical Society, so that we could spend more time together as a family. John, Michele, Dave, and Maryann called almost every day. One or two of them were home each weekend.

We had become so aware of how much we meant to each other. We were less selfish, less concerned about ourselves and our own needs. We were waking up to how important we were to each other; how important Chris was to us. I thought we had known that before, but Chris's illness made everything clearer. We savored everything we did together as though we were doing them for the last time. Perhaps that is why, so many years later our memory of events is still crystal clear.

But, in spite of our support, Chris was still alone. He was the one who had cancer, he had the pain, and at the very least, it was he who had to face experimental Interleukin II chemotherapy. But emotionally, in his quiet introspective way, Chris was dealing with the reality of his cancer. In his soul, he was gathering strength for the ordeal ahead.

As the summer wore on, my anxiety became unbearable because the cancer was going unchecked. No other form of medicine could be used to stop the spread of cancer while we waited for NCI to respond and of course to accept him. There was no doubt in our minds, at least consciously, that Chris would be a candidate for Interleukin II. However, that was not helping Chris now while we waited. We knew that the cancer was advancing because his activities were greatly limited due to the increased pain in his back.

My friend, Terese encouraged me to investigate non-traditional options for fighting cancer. One such option was a relaxation tape which cancer patients use while getting chemotherapy or radiation. Chris agreed to try the tape even though he was a bit skeptical that it would help but he did listen to the tape before dinner each evening.

I also discovered a book, *Returned to Life*, written by Dr. Satillaro, a physician who had metastatic prostate cancer. The author wrote of his complete remission after completely changing his diet to the macrobiotic diet. I received more information about macrobiotics in a health food store. Further, I learned that a physician in a Chicago suburb prescribed the macrobiotic diet to many of his patients because he, like Dr. Satillaro, attributed his return to health from a fatal disease to the macrobiotic diet. Chris was skeptical of this approach and only reluctantly agreed to a consultation with the doctor.

The physician was very pleased that Chris was applying for

the Interleukin II program. He believed that Interleukin along with the macrobiotic diet would save Chris's life. In fact, he said that in the future, traditional medical treatment and the macrobiotic diet or another form of nutritional regimen would be the prescribed treatment for cancer.

We left his office with information, recipes, and most of all, hope. Chris liked what he heard and was willing to try the new approach. Hooray! Jack and I had already decided that if Chris went on the diet, we would too; it was the only way it would work for Chris. We wanted to support him. Anything, anything to help Chris.

The next day armed with a cook book I began to prepare macrobiotic meals. The diet was very different and difficult to adjust to because the flavors were so alien to our taste buds. The recipes were so foreign to me that I had to make repeated phone calls to the doctor's nurse who was always very helpful and encouraging. I spent most of the day cooking, and most of the time Chris did not eat very much of whatever I cooked. In three weeks he lost ten pounds.

Dr. Paul had no problem with the diet, but he was concerned that Chris had lost weight. He wanted Chris to be at optimal weight when Interleukin II treatment was started because Chris would lose weight during the treatment. In addition, Maryann and Dave were not convinced that this diet would help Chris, and thought Chris might be going through needless discomfort. Chris himself was not convinced that the diet would help him, because he told me he did not want to stay on the diet. I reluctantly agreed and we returned to our regular diet. Perhaps he needed more encouragement. Perhaps if he had stayed on it he would have gone into remission. We will never know.

In the beginning of the summer, he was still able to sleep in his bed because the egg crate over his mattress provided some comfort. But many times, I'd come down in the morning to find him asleep on the sofa. I knew the pain must have been very bad. I would serve him breakfast on a tray so that he would not have to walk to the table and sit on a straight back chair. After breakfast he sat for an hour as he tried to summon strength to climb the stairs so that he could shower and dress.

He seemed to have aged. His once animated happy face was thin and pale now. His eyes were a mirror for the pain and grief he was enduring. No longer did he walk with a sure firm bounce to his step. He walked very slowly now as someone does that is in constant pain. The sight of my son in such failing health was agony. Moreover, I had to hope against hope that he would not get worse.

By the middle of summer, Chris was no longer able to sleep in his bed because it was too painful for him to lie flat on his back. He began to sleep sitting up on the family room sofa. Each night I did whatever I could to make him comfortable. I'd carefully position six or seven soft down pillows around him, behind his back and head, under his arms and his knees and place a couple close to him in case he needed more. One morning, after a particularly painful night, Chris said, "I wish I had one of those lounge chairs that recline, like a Lazy Boy chair. I think it would be so comfortable."

He said it with such a pained and wistful look, that I immediately said, "Then we'll get one for you." I would have carted it in on my back if it would have meant relieving some of his suffering.

But Chris immediately responded with anger and said, "No. I don't want you to buy one. It won't fit in this room." As though that was of paramount importance. At this point he thought his pain would soon be relieved by his admission into the Interleukin protocol, and so he didn't want to give in and accept any changes.

I argued with him that we could easily move out one of the other chairs. But he dug in his heels and became adamant that he didn't want one, and I should not buy one. Regretfully, I listened to him. But that was one time that I wish with all my heart that I had not. I should have simply bought one and had it delivered. I'm sure that upon seeing it and realizing the degree of comfort it would provide that he would have changed his mind. Why didn't I? Instead I deferred to him because I wanted him to be in charge.

Each night, after getting Chris comfortable with pillows, we'd watch Jay Leno or Letterman, his favorites. They took his mind off his own problems and gave us something to laugh about. Most nights after giving him a pill for pain, I'd stay up, and we would talk about our concerns. Nighttime was a low point for Chris. It was a time when he became truly aware of his condition. I sensed his utter loneliness and separation. The agony for me was that I could not restore his life. But I was determined to walk the journey with him so that he would be less alone and less afraid.

In those quiet hours that the two of us spent on the sofa, Chris shared his thoughts and feelings with me. He talked about Ann and how devastating the breakup had been for him. He discussed his depression and the counseling that helped him to deal with the breakup. He still thought about her and wondered how her life was going. He talked about the pain of perhaps having to give up his dreams. We talked about family issues. Chris told me what he hoped for his two sisters and his brother.

One evening I referred to what he was going through as suffering and he replied, "Mom, Jesus suffered; I'm in pain." He didn't equate what he was going through with what Jesus endured.

Frequently Chris would say, "Mom, what are you feeling?" or, "Tell me what you're worried about." I was in a difficult position because I did not want to add to his burden but I was an open book. One night he said, "Mom, I feel terrible about what's happening to this family. Look at how your face has changed. You're so sad."

I remember saying, "Whatever happens to you touches and affects all of us. That's just the way it is, Chris."

I told him of my concern and frustration about the delay hearing from NCI. I shared insights and worries about aspects of his care and treatment. He and I worried that even if he did survive, the radiation treatments might make him sterile. I told him about my concerns for Maryann, Michele, and John. We talked about things we would change if we could. One night I apologized for an incident that had happened years before when Chris was a teenager. I had slapped his face because he had mouthed off. I did not believe in physical punishment and the memory of that slap was still with me and shamed me. Chris shrugged it off saying, "Mom, if I started apologizing to you for all the times I mouthed off to you, we'd be here all night."

Those hours together meant so much to Chris and me. Soul to soul we grieved for ourselves, for our losses, for each other. We cried together, sensing the ordeals to come. We mourned for the years we would not have together, for the children he would not have, for the future that seemed so threatened. I was able to enter his world and he was able to enter mine. I wanted to be present to him so he would be less alone, and I hoped, less afraid. Through those hours of sharing, our spirits drew strength from one another and bonded for eternity.

Journal Entry • August 2, 1986

What will I die of if my son dies of cancer? Will I die of a broken heart? Will I go stark raving mad? Or will I die of the pain of seeing Chris die? What's harder breathing in or just giving up and breathing out? I know we are all terminal but this is obscene. Parents die first – not children. The reverse is obscene. I brought him into this world. Will it be my task to help him out of it – to help him to die? Why Lord? Why? Why? Why? I put so much value on Chris's life and so little on mine. I would gladly take his place. Easier for me to die than to watch my son die. It's the greatest pain on earth. My heart is being wrenched out of my body.

Jack too is in great pain. I go upstairs to find him sitting in our room reading the Book of Job with whom he identifies. He's looking for consolation, understanding, and answers. One day he looked at me with a pained and bewildered expression and said, "Therese, there are so many people praying for Chris, but he's not

getting better, he's getting worse. Where are all the prayers going?"
I had no answer!

Terese F. says there are miracles for everyone — enough for
everyone — especially for Chris and us. I want to believe that.

Each day was harder than the day before. Some days I did
not cry at all, and other days I cried everywhere: in church, in
the grocery store, in the car. Tears came so often that sometimes
I did not know that I had been crying until I touched my face
and found it was wet. It was difficult to sleep through the night.
I was depressed, sad, scared, terrified, confused and angry.
It was so painful to see Chris in pain — ten months of pain!

During those months, my emotions changed hourly — from
prayerful hope, to doubt, to despair and desperation and
frequently to anger and rage at God. I tried bargaining with
God, pleading with Him to take me instead. I asked if He was
punishing me. He knew that losing any of my children was
the worst pain I would ever have to endure.

I was angry at medicine, angry with NCI and most of all I
was angry with God. Everything we tried had failed and Chris
was getting sicker. One afternoon, after we received the results
of another test showing increased metastasis, I went out to the
patio, grabbed a broom, and started to sweep the patio. Anger,
fear, and rage poured out of me with each sweep of the broom.
Tears as big as raindrops kept falling and wetting the concrete.
As I swept, I raged at God. "Is this what You want? Don't You
have enough young men in heaven? Do You need Chris too?
We need him more than You do! He has so much to give! Don't
take him now. You'll have him soon enough. If You have to
take someone, take me not my son. How can You do this to
Chris? Why aren't You helping him? You don't love us. You help
others but You are not helping us. I don't even think You hear
me or care that Chris is suffering. What kind of God are You?"

I had always feared God the Father, the First Person of the
Blessed Trinity: the angry, vengeful God of the Old Testament.

Sixteen years of Catholic education had fostered that image of God. He was the unbending tyrant, with absolute power of life and death. He performed miracles if He wanted to. But He was not helping Chris. He did not care, or feel any compassion for us. I believed He was punishing me.

I had shared my feelings with my friend, Terese, a fellow counselor and former nun. We met for coffee at 7 a.m. once a week for most of the months that Chris was sick. It was an hour a week that really helped me and the only time each week when I met with a friend. She was more than just my friend and confidante. She inspired me to look within for answers and challenged me to grow. Terese encouraged me to deal with all the issues that were coming up because of Chris's illness. She suggested that I talk to Anne, a gifted young woman that she thought might help me. Reluctantly I agreed.

After listening to me for a few minutes and becoming aware of my anger toward God, Anne suggested that I do a Gestalt empty chair technique with God. It is a method with which I was familiar. It is used to release and work through emotions that one has toward another person. It involves symbolically placing the person with whom one has a problem in a chair opposite from the one where one is sitting. One speaks to the empty chair as though that person is actually sitting there. After one has released all the feelings and judgments that arise, one must change chairs and become the other person and speak from that person's perspective and point of view. One switches chairs as often as needed until one feels one has reached a new awareness and understanding of the situation.

At Anne's request and with reluctance and a heavy heart, I symbolically placed God, the Father, in the chair opposite the chair in which I sat. Emotions immediately flooded to the surface. All the pent up anger and rage that I had tried to control for so long came out in torrents of tears. I vented my fury at God. Between sobs, I angrily voiced my fear that Chris was dying and He, God, wasn't helping. I raged at Him and accused

Him of not caring. "Chris is getting sicker and he will die unless You help him and still You turn a deaf ear. You knew that taking one of my children was the worst thing You could do to me and You are doing it anyway. We have all been praying and begging You and You refuse to hear us. Why are You punishing us? You took my two-year-old sister. How can You be a loving God when You take children away from their parents! What kind of a God are You?"

I poured out my bitterness. I refused to change chairs and to "become" God. Angrily I told Anne I wanted no part of being God. I didn't want to hear what He had to say. I didn't want to understand, to be placated. I wanted to stay angry with Him. I continued to rage at Him. Finally, when I was emotionally spent, Anne said again that I had to change chairs.

Still sobbing I changed chairs and became God, the Father. I heard myself say the words that I have never forgotten and that changed my life: "From the beginning of time I have created out of love. Therese, I love you and I love Chris. I am not punishing you through Chris. I love Chris more than you do. I am not killing Chris. His body is no longer able to sustain him. I didn't will or cause his cancer. His body doesn't have the ability to fight off the cancer. I didn't will this any more than I willed your little sister, Gen, to die of pneumonia."

The words that continued to pour out of my mouth were full of love and kindness. The words shocked me. They did not seem to be coming from me. Years later I realized that the words came from deep within my soul where I had always known the truth. I do not consciously remember all the words I spoke as "God", but the experience changed me and became a turning point.

I left Anne's home feeling peaceful and serene. No longer did I feel anger toward God because I no longer blamed Him for Chris's cancer and our pain. I could feel God's love for me. Before the empty chair technique with God, it seemed to me that my prayers were blocked from reaching Him. Afterwards, I felt and still feel an openness of communication, a friendship that I had never before experienced. God was listening to me! Much later, I realized it was I who had been blocking God. The chair technique was the vehicle that helped me to release my anger and fear and left a space for grace to enter. Instead of demanding that God do what I wanted Him to do for Chris, I could be open to hearing what God wanted of me.

In the days after the empty chair technique, as I marveled at what had happened, I began to look at our situation differently. Could it be that God had other plans for Chris? I came face to face with a power that superceded all my motherly hopes and dreams for a long fruitful life for my son. It was a moment of hopelessness and of defeat and also a moment of transcendent awareness - a turning point. I had been led to it, kicking and screaming, shaking my fist in rage at God. I had been knocked to my knees. At the same time I was drawn into mystery. I was allowed to glimpse deeper possibilities - that there are forces in motion, beyond our human awareness and understanding that affect and determine what happens on the human level.

Could it be that even while we live on this human level, we are at the same time participants in the spiritual plane, the realm of the soul. Could it be that when the soul's work is finished here, it moves on? Perhaps even before the soul comes to earth it already has set a time for leaving it.

As a Christian I had always believed in the life of the spirit and eternal life. But until that moment I had been merely paying lip service to it. This was the moment of truth in which I was being called to live my belief. I acknowledged that I did not understand the great spiritual forces at work in Chris's life, in any of our lives. Who could comprehend God's broad and perfect plan for us? I resigned myself to the fact that God was asking me to be open to His plan for Chris and for our family. I did not know what His plan was but through God's grace and with great apprehension, I slowly began to accept His will. This spiritual "yes" seemed to help me as we continued to receive bad news about Chris's condition. The pain and fear were still very real but at the same time something had changed. My soul was at peace.

Gradually, I began to look at our situation with a new understanding. The events that I blamed God for, I now saw as human failings, not as the will of God. I understood that Dr. Smith's failure to diagnose Chris's pain as cancer in October of 1985 was a human error, not the hand of God. When National Cancer Institute gave Jack permission to have Chris continue with radiation to the spine, it was NCI's poor communication that failed to warn Jack that if radiation were repeated, Chris would have to wait another month before being allowed to come to NCI. When Dr. Rosenberg turned Chris down, it was because the tingling and numbness in his thighs were indications of spinal cord involvement. The treatment itself causes swelling; therefore, Interleukin could have caused paralysis. Further, Interleukin causes a response with undifferentiated cancer cells, and Chris's were differentiated. By the time Dr. Martin (fictitious name) told us in October that there was no medical hope of Chris recovering, I was better prepared to accept it. I still hoped and prayed daily for a miracle. But at this point, I was open to understanding that God was not willing Chris's death.

⚡ 6 ⚡

CRUCIBLE

At last Chris had an appointment with National Cancer Institute in Washington D.C. where he was to be inter viewed and examined by Dr. Rosenburg. Unfortunately, because of the second set of radiation treatments, his appointment had been delayed a month. Chris was anxious now to regain the ten pounds he had lost while on the macrobiotic diet, because he wanted to be strong and healthy when he started the protocol. Our grave concern was that Chris had begun to feel tingling in his thighs causing him to lose strength in his legs. We were afraid to know what that signified and how it would affect his eligibility.

Jack and Chris were going without me. I would accompany Chris when he went to Washington for the actual chemotherapy and remain with him for the weeks he would have to be there. But I rode in to Chicago with them to spend the night with my parents rather than to wait alone.

We had lunch with Mom and Dad, and Dad or Nanno as our children called him, regaled Chris with stories of his youth and had Chris laughing. Chris and Dad had always had a special relationship due to their similar interests. He and Mom were devastated that Chris had cancer, but aside from praying for his recovery, there was little they could do. But at that moment they could make him laugh, serve him his favorite Italian foods, kiss and hug him and bless him on his way.

Jack and Chris were to call us after the interview with Dr. Rosenburg. My parents and I drove to the Shrine of St. Jude, patron saint of hopeless or difficult cases, to pray that Chris would be accepted into the Interleukin II program. And then there was nothing left to do but to return home and wait for the call.

Finally, Chris called and explained that he and eleven others had been interviewed by a resident and then by Dr. Rosenburg, whom Chris said had been very nice. He asked many questions, checked and reviewed his chart, and then asked about the tingling in his thighs that Christopher had been experiencing for the last few weeks. Chris told him he didn't know what was causing the tingling, and Dr. Rosenburg said he didn't know either, but he didn't like it. He told Chris to go home and they would call him with the results the following week.

Again I had a sinking, visceral feeling that he was going to be turned down. I told Mom and Dad that if he were turned down, that would be the end. They looked blank, unwilling to understand what I was saying.

We returned home and again we waited anxiously. Jack called Dr. Paul, and gave him his impressions of the interview with Dr. Rosenburg, and told him he feared Chris would be rejected. But Dr. Paul said no, they could not be that selective, surely they would take him. His response was encouraging, because he had worked with Dr. Rosenburg and understood the process of selection.

A long week later, while Jack and I were attending a prayer service, Chris received the devastating phone call from NCI telling him that he had been rejected for the Interleukin II protocol, because he did not fit the criteria. He had been alone when he received the catastrophic news. When we came home, Chris told us that he had been turned down. NCI was concerned that the tingling sensation in his thighs meant that the cancer had spread to the spinal canal.

We had spent the summer waiting, dreading, and fearing that the cancer was spreading. In the beginning of our communication with NCI, we had been told that they would not consider him unless or until there was metastases to soft tissue. Now he was being turned down because there was too much metastasis. Yet, twice during that summer we had sent x-rays, MRIs, bone scans, and blood work to NCI. They must have seen the progression of the cancer. Couldn't they have called him at just the right time? Couldn't they have made clear to us that, if Chris had the second course of radiation, he would have to wait another month? What were we to do now? Months had been lost because we had pinned all of our hopes on NCI. Words cannot describe the depths of our sorrow, our sense of failure, our anger, the gut wrenching fear that Chris would die.

The next morning Jack called Dr. Paul to inform him that Chris had been rejected by NCI. He expressed surprise and disappointment. He said surely then, Chris could get into one of the other centers that were using Interleukin II. He mentioned Loyola Medical center in Chicago, City of Hope, and several others. Jack immediately contacted each one of the centers. What he learned turned my blood to ice. All of the centers had shut down their Interleukin II studies. They believed it was a temporary shut down, but they could not say when the study would be accepting patients. We spent the next three weeks making calls to them to ask when they were going to reopen. Their answers were evasive. We didn't know where to turn.

Finally, our son-in-law, David called Loyola, and was able to get through to a colleague who was willing to provide clarification. David told him about his young brother-in-law and appealed to him for help. He said we needed some honesty and clarification as to why the Interleukin II study was shut down and when it would reopen. The physician revealed that all the studies were down because there was a problem with the culture medium. Patients who had received Interleukin from the culture had contracted hepatitis. Consequently, they had shut down the studies until the problem was resolved. All the outlying centers were receiving Interleukin from the same source, consequently, all were shut down. Too late, we became aware that we had wasted more precious time trying to get Chris into the protocol. There was no more time to waste.

Chris called Dr. Paul and related what we had learned about the centers. The plan was that, if Chris couldn't get into one of the outlying centers, then Chris would begin another form of chemotherapy at the university hospital where Dr. Paul was head of oncology. Now an appointment for the second week of October was made. We just hoped and prayed that the cancer would respond. However, our hopes were sinking with each passing day. It was now the end of September.

Chris's pain had been increasing steadily all summer long. As it did, Chris tried stronger and stronger pain relievers; however, none of them worked for any length of time, not even the Brompton cocktail, a mixture of potent pain relievers that are often given to cancer patients. It made Chris very groggy and nauseated; but even that didn't give him much relief from pain or help him to get a few hours of restful sleep. There seemed to be no relief from the pain.

The weekend of October Third, when Michele came home to celebrate her birthday, Chris was having difficulty walking. What could this mean? We were terrified. We were marking time, holding our breath until Chris would have his appointment with Dr. Paul. But we knew that Chris's health was plummeting.

I cried quietly as I watched from the kitchen window as he slowly, painfully made his way out to the backyard. He looked older that twenty-two. He walked with his shoulders bent forward, trying with each step to protect his fragile spine from feeling the impact with the ground. In my heart I knew what he was doing. He was walking in the garden for the last time, the garden that he had played in since he was four.

I remembered the years when I had stood at this same window and watched contentedly as he and John played with their trucks, romped with our dog, had noisy snowball fights, and built snowmen. And now it was over. Twenty-two years had fled by.

I wished I could do it over – more consciously. I wished I had spent my time consciously focused on being with my children, having fun and creating joy filled memories, and less time on being a conscientious homemaker. So many years had been taken for granted. I had so many unshed tears and so much grief inside of me that I could barely breathe.

I watched him for the last time as he walked slowly and painfully all the way to the back of the yard where he and John played with their trucks, then over to the stone wall and steps that he and John had constructed, then to the side garden that he had helped to plant. He made a slow, complete circle, remembering and looking at everything as if for the last time, and saying goodbye. He came back into the house, and quietly sat down in the family room alone with his thoughts. My brave son was dealing with his reality.

We had planned to celebrate Michele's birthday by going out to dinner together, but now Chris said he couldn't go. Sitting in a straight back chair in a restaurant would be too painful, he said. I think he also realized that walking had become extremely painful. But he insisted that we go on with our plans.

Michele left on Sunday, and by that evening Christopher had so much difficulty walking that the three of us decided that he should try walking with a cane. For the next two days Chris walked with the help of the cane, but he didn't even try using the stairs; they were beyond his efforts with or without the use of a cane. He was confined now to the first floor.

For the past two months, I had been setting an alarm clock to wake me at night, so that I could give Chris the pain medication on time. Now that he was walking with a cane, I wanted to be close by where I would hear him if he called. We brought down a mattress; laid it on the living room floor, and I slept there.

After getting Chris set for the night and after talking and praying together, I would go into the living room to toss and turn until the alarm went off. My waking reality had become worse than the nightmares that I was having. There were many factors that contributed to an overall exhaustion of my body and of my spirit.

On Tuesday evening, October 5, Chris and I were alone because Jack was attending a medical meeting. Around 7:00

p.m. Chris rose from the sofa, and with the aid of his cane, slowly walked to the bathroom. As he came back into the family room, he suddenly fell to the floor. His legs had given out. In shock and horror, I jumped up to help him, but he shouted at me to leave him alone. Using his arms, he backed himself up against the desk and sat there on the floor. The two of us stared at each other barely breathing, saying nothing, as the realization penetrated our brains and our souls. We knew! Something irrevocable had happened. He could no longer walk. Finally, he made his way to the sofa half-crawling, half-standing. I sat frozen and helpless, silently screaming at this new, vile assault on Chris. How much more would he have to endure?

When Jack returned, we told him the terrible thing that had befallen us. The three of us were numb, overwhelmed by panic, grief, rage, and blinding despair. Chris was paralyzed! Our son was paralyzed! We had no time to recover from the shock. For Chris's sake, we forced ourselves to think. Woodenly, we talked about needing a wheelchair so that Chris could get to the bathroom. Chris needed to call Dr. Paul immediately to move up the admission appointment to the university hospital. We needed to call Maryann, Michele, and John.

The next morning Jack brought home a wheelchair. Chris learned how to transfer his weight from the sofa to the wheelchair, but the shift intensified the already almost unbearable pain. I could not lift Chris, so Jack came home as often as possible during the day in order to lift Chris into the wheelchair, take him to the bathroom, and then help him back to the sofa.

That week was one of the worst weeks of our lives up to that point. Chris was overwhelmed by his helplessness. So far he had been able to handle everything that had happened to him. He had still been able to look ahead. The loss of his legs had taken him over the edge. He was terrified, in despair that he would not recover.

Helplessness was worst that any pain he had to endure. Frustrated and racked with pain, he raged at Jack and me. We couldn't do anything right. He was critical and insulting as he vented his rage. He didn't want any help, but he needed assistance for almost everything. He became angry if we tried to do more than he asked us to do. I seemed to be hovering over him in anticipation of his needs. He hated that. It only increased his sense of helplessness.

He had planned to get a hair cut the week before he became paralyzed, but he had not gone because of the pain, and because he had lacked the energy to go. Now he complained that his hair was too long. When I suggested that I ask his barber to make a house call, he flatly refused. I knew he hated his helplessness and did not want anyone feeling sorry for him.

He asked me to wash his hair at the kitchen sink as he sat in the wheelchair. I bought a plastic cape and a tray and tried to wash his hair without hurting him. He had very little mobility in his upper body because of the pain in his back. I tried to keep him dry but ended up making a mess of both of us and of the kitchen floor. I came away shaken, with a dawning awareness of what it means to care for a handicapped person. Chris was angry with me, and I was angry with Chris because he was angry with me. I understood what he was feeling, but at the same time, I didn't know how to help him any differently. Damn this whole deplorable direction our lives had taken. Damn cancer; damn medicine and NCI; damn us all for our delays, misplaced trust, and obviously wrong decisions. At that moment I felt beaten and close to exhaustion.

Fortunately, and with God's grace, the feeling passed, and by the weekend, I was again focused on getting Chris to the hospital on Monday morning so that he could receive help. Chris was still angry, but the outbursts had ceased. All of us were feeling deep emotional pain as we grieved Chris's earlier life when he was healthy and happy and free.

We went to the hospital on Monday morning with the idea that Chris would be there primarily to begin chemotherapy. We also knew that he would be having a surgical procedure to place a Hickman catheter into the subclavein vein in his chest. Chris would be getting a small but steady dose of chemo through the port in the catheter rather than the usual powerful doses by injection. He would be in the hospital for about three days.

We somehow managed to get Chris into the front seat of the car for the three and half-hour trip. We drove to the medical complex, and pulled into one of the wide parking spaces in front of the entry that were reserved for the handicapped. I was grateful for that kindness. I had not realized how difficult it is to help a handicapped person in and out of a car. A normal parking space does not allow one to fully open the door in order to place a wheel chair along side.

I went into the lobby to get a wheelchair. It was old, an institutional wooden chair with a high back, a sad looking wheelchair that had been around for a long time. We registered in a reception area that was crowded with people and television sets. Chris wheeled his chair to a corner that was out of the way and sat there forlornly.

A sign pointed to a chapel. Feeling a strong desire to pray alone for a few minutes, I told Jack and Chris that I would be in the chapel if Chris was called.

The small non-sectarian chapel was serenely quiet and a world removed from the crowded reception area. There was only room for a few rows of pews and a small altar behind which was an illuminated window simulating stained glass with a vertical design that resembled skyscrapers. I sat in the empty chapel praying for Chris.

For several weeks I had been grappling with the fear that if Chris died, he would go into a void, a dark abyss before he would be in the presence of God. That recurring image caused me real distress, because I couldn't bear the thought that Chris would be frightened and alone. At that point, I didn't know what happened at the moment of death. I had not yet read any accounts of near death experiences.

I sat absently gazing at the light coming in through the contemporary stained glass window. As the light poured through every prism of the glass, I suddenly became aware that there was no darkness, no abyss. There was no space in which God was not present. Just as the light lit up all of the parts of the window, so too God's presence was everywhere. Chris would not go into darkness and nothingness. He would go directly into the arms of Jesus, because there was only light!

It was a wonderful revelation, reminding me that the Lord understood and had kindly helped me to overcome the obstacle to my understanding. A gift for broken me. After those few moments in the chapel, I stopped fearing that Chris would go into darkness. I returned to the reception area with a sense that God was with us. He was not taking away our ordeal, but He was with us.

Finally Chris was called. We went from department to department as Christopher had one test after another. Eventually, he was brought upstairs to the oncology floor where he was put into a room. What was our young son doing here on the oncology floor? It was beyond comprehension and too much to accept!

I looked at Chris paralyzed and sad in a hospital bed. A far cry from my once handsome and energetic son. I recalled how happy and handsome he looked in his tux at Maryann's wedding. I remember when he walked me down the isle, before I sat down, he kissed me on the cheek. It was a gesture that touched me, because he was not demonstrative, especially in public. He had missed the rehearsal dinner the night before, because he had already started his summer job at a local manufacturing plant. I was disappointed that he was not there, but I knew there would be many other times in the future when he would celebrate with us. Little did I know, that just a few short months later, he would be on the oncology floor fighting for his life and his future.

Shortly after he was settled, several interns and residents came in to see Chris. They were amazed, shocked that he couldn't walk. Apparently, Dr. Paul had not understood when Chris spoke to him, or perhaps he simply had not told his interns and residents of his condition.

Before addressing the cancer, the placement of the Hickman catheter, or starting chemotherapy, the cause of the paralysis had to be determined. A tumor in the spinal canal was suspected. It was their hope that he could have surgery to reverse the paralysis. He would need to have a mylegram to determine the location and size of the tumor. Chris was very willing to go through the procedure and we gratefully agreed to the change in plans. We spent the afternoon waiting while arrangements were made for Chris to have the procedure.

The week before this Chris had said little about the paralysis. Instead his terror and frustration had been expressed through rage and anger. Now he was being told that perhaps the paralysis was reversible and he would be able to walk again. Now, in his room, the two of us were alone. He looked at me with tears in his eyes and said, "Mom, could I have a hug?" I leaned over his bed and put my arms around him. He cried as he said, "Oh Mom, just pray that they can reverse this, that I can get my legs back, that I can walk again." The two of us hugged each other and sobbed.

Finally, Christopher was taken down to the large new wing where the mylegram was to be done. Maryann and Dave joined Jack and me, and the four of us sat in the waiting room for hours. Every once in a while, Dave would go in to see how the mylegram was progressing. Each time he came out, I would look at his closed and guarded face. Dave didn't tell us how bad things were, but as time wore on, Jack and I knew the news was bad.

A mylegram procedure involves injecting dye into the spinal canal. If the spinal canal is clear of tumor, the dye will spread throughout the canal and will be visible on a screen. If there is a block due to a tumor, the dye cannot enter the canal, and therefore the dye will not be seen on the screen. It took hours for Chris to go through the procedure for which he was given some pain medication, but not general anesthesia. Chris was awake and undergoing excruciating pain. Later, with tears in his eyes, Dave told us what Chris had endured. The physician who did the procedure told Dave that he was awed by Chris's courage, and by his determination to continue with the procedure in spite of the incredible pain that he had to endure as time after time the dye was injected into the spinal canal.

The procedure started at the mid-point of the canal. Each time the dye was injected it shot back; since the spinal canal was filled with tumor there was no place for it to go. The needle would be withdrawn and injected higher up the spine with the same result. They continued to inject the dye higher and higher until the base of the neck was reached before the dye had a place to enter. The same procedure was followed, starting at the base of the spine. The dye spread upward in the canal until it reached the tumor. That was the method through which the length of the blockage was determined.

The pain Chris suffered during those five excruciating hours is unimaginable. It was only a foreshadowing of what was to come in the months ahead. Now, seventeen years later, the images are still so vivid and strong that it seems as though it has just happened and I am moved to tears. But now the tears are not only for Chris, but for all children who are suffering from catastrophic illness.

Finally, at 11:00 p.m., one of the physicians came to give us the results. Chris had eight inches of cancerous tumor in his spinal canal. If the tumor were smaller, they could do surgery and perhaps put in a steel rod that would reinforce the spine. As it was, eight inches of tumor was a tremendous amount to remove. However, the resident did not say it was impossible, further, he said that Christopher wanted to go ahead with the surgery. The decision to operate would be made by the surgeon whom we were told was very reticent to operate, because it would require fifteen hours of surgery. Because of blood loss, three-quarters of Chris's blood supply would have to be replaced. At that point, the physician said, anything could go wrong. We were horror stricken at the thought of Christopher undergoing fifteen hours of surgery, losing three-quarters of his blood supply, and having to wear a brace for a year. But yet, we did not say no. It had to be Chris's decision. If Christopher wanted to do this, if this was the only chance that he had, we would support him.

It wasn't until 11:30 p.m. that Christopher was taken to a room in the neurosurgical wing where he would remain because he was paralyzed. All procedures could be taken care of from there. We were only able to see him for a brief moment before a team of nurses came in to take care of him. He was in intense pain; but even worse than the physical pain was the reality of his condition.

We kissed him and with broken hearts we reluctantly left and checked into a nearby hotel. We were too sick at heart to eat; all we wanted was a glass of wine. As we sat in the bar Jack and I slowly fell apart, crying and mourning the loss of our beautiful son. Christopher was going to die!

Early the next morning we returned to the hospital in dread of what we were about to hear from the neurosurgeon who would determine if surgery was to be done. Dr. Martin told us point blank that he would not do the surgery, because he believed that Chris would not survive it. He said that eight inches of tumor was impossible to remove, not only because of the extent of the tumor, but also because of its placement in the spinal canal. Chris's tumor was growing between the spinal cord and the spine in the canal, compressing the cord, causing paralysis. There was no way that the tumor could be removed by going through his back. Not only was there an eight inch tumor in the spinal canal, it was also facing the wrong way.

Another devastating blow. Every door that we tried to open was slammed in our faces. Everything we tried was to no avail. It was as though God Himself was calling Chris. In spite of the fact that he was only twenty-two and robust; in spite of the fact that we tried to get him into National Cancer Institute; nothing was working for him. It seemed that no matter what we did, or tried to do, our efforts were fruitless. It was so frightening to come face to face with the mystifying forces that were determining how Chris's life would proceed. And yet, when Dr. Martin, after telling us that he could not do the surgery, told us of another procedure that might work, all of us agreed – do it!

The procedure is emolization. He recommended an invasive radiologist, an expert at this procedure. It involved threading a catheter through the femoral artery to the aorta and then into the site where the tumor mass was compressing the spinal cord. A substance would be injected through the catheter that would destroy the blood supply to the tumor, thus causing the tumor to shrink. By taking pressure off the spinal cord, perhaps feeling and motion would be restored to Chris's legs. It was his only hope.

Chris readily agreed to have emolization. He would do anything to walk again. He would be transferred by ambulance to the medical complex in Madison the next day; have the procedure on Thursday, and return to the hospital in Milwaukee on Friday.

Dr. Martin had expedited Chris's registration and admission into the hospital in Madison; and he was quickly taken to his room. He was now receiving four milligrams per hour of intravenous morphine drip through a catheter in his arm, because the intense pain could only be alleviated by morphine. Jack and I were grateful that at least he was no longer experiencing physical pain, but Chris's emotional pain could not be alleviated.

The invasive radiologist came in with his team and explained the procedure to us. Thankfully it would be painless. The next day, while Chris had the procedure we prayed for a miracle. That evening, after the procedure, the radiologist and his nurse came into Chris's room and asked if he could feel anything more in his legs than the tingling that he had felt before. Sadly, Chris had to say, "No."

The next morning the doctor came in again and asked Chris

if he had any more feeling in his legs. Chris shook his head, "No, I have less feeling than I did before." The procedure had been unsuccessful. Chris would not walk again. Brokenhearted and consumed by depression we made the sad trip back to the medical complex in Milwaukee, Christopher by ambulance and Jack and I in our car.

The medical team had decided that Christopher should have a series of radiation treatments on his spinal canal in the hope it would reduce and eliminate the tumor. However, from our past experience with radiation, we didn't have much hope that radiation would affect the tumor. The plan was to continue the radiation daily until he received a total of twenty-one treatments. Then he would have surgery to place the Hickman catheter and be released. Chris would remain in the hospital during that time, and I would remain in Milwaukee with Chris, and stay with Maryann and Dave. But Jack had to return to his practice.

There was so much pent up emotion in me, but I held back. I was afraid to let go for fear I would fall apart. Instead I fell into bloodless depression and sadness. I had no interest in myself or my health. I didn't care if I lived or died except as it would affect Chris. I was in a suspended state as I moved like an inmate on death row, without hope, therefore without energy or life force.

Each morning at Maryann's house I awoke to depression and sadness that permeated every cell. I moved in the same world as everyone else, but lived in a world apart, alone, consumed by my own fears and grief, a shadow figure detached from the surroundings, an automaton that walked down corridors, and lost track of time. I lived in my thoughts, my head filled with images of my beautiful, young son, paralyzed in a hospital bed, helpless and depressed, his face sad and ashen, his head and arm movements slow and deliberate, his once beautiful eyes now veiled and full of sorrow, showing no interest, as though his life were already over. I visualized and pined for the healthy, vibrant son who fully engaged life.

It was difficult for Chris to be alone. So I arrived early each morning and stayed until 9 p.m., simply sitting with him, because most of the time he did not want to talk. I'd look out across the landscaped hospital complex to a beautiful wooded area. It was October and the leaves were brilliant shades of red and yellow. In my joyless state it hurt to look at them because they were so beautiful. I would have preferred it to be bitterly cold and rainy and as miserable outside as I was feeling on the inside. Although we never spoke of it, Christopher had the same reaction. He did not want the blinds open all the way. I had to adjust them so that he could look out but not see the trees.

One morning I entered his room to find that a trapeze had been placed over his bed to aid him in lifting himself. Chris had his arms on the trapeze; his head resting on his hands. As I walked in, he looked up at me and his eyes filled with tears. It was breaking his heart to find himself in this devastating situation. He who had always been so independent was now totally dependent upon others. Cancer, now paralysis, what else would he have to face? His hope that he would return to the life he loved was gone, and all that lay ahead was pain, loss, and death. I read it on his face as I looked at him. We held hands as we silently cried together. Where would it end?

Every day he was taken for radiation treatment and received physical therapy. It took hours for him to go back and forth. He had to be placed on a hospital cart, wait for an aid to take him there, then wait to be brought back. Once he lay on a cart for an hour because the aid forgot to come for him. He spent interminable periods of time waiting.

I too waited. Since Chris's surgery in February, I had spent days waiting in hospital corridors, waiting rooms, and lobbies. Although I was there for twelve hours a day, there were many hours when I couldn't see Chris because he was in radiation or in physical therapy. I'd wait outside of his room leaning against a wall in a trance, almost catatonic, detached from my physical self, unaware of tiredness or hunger or that I had been crying until I'd discover that my face was wet.

Chris had become the focus for the family, and each of us did our best to rally around him. Michele, John, and Jack visited every weekend. Maryann brought him homemade snacks, made his room homey and comfortable with family pictures, and aware of his love for sunsets, she hung a large picture of a sunset across from his bed. Several times a day she and Dave would slip up to Chris's room for a quick visit. She brought eleven-month old David to the hospital to visit Chris hoping that seeing little David would cheer him up. But each time that Chris saw David was more painful than the last. One night he said, "All I want to do is to be with that little boy. And I know I won't see him grow up." A few days later, close to tears he said, "Please ask Maryann not to bring David here any more. It's too hard to see him. He reminds me of everything I will be missing."

I repeated Chris's request to Maryann. However, Maryann and Dave, since it was almost Halloween, planned to dress David in a costume and surprise Chris. I had mixed emotions about this but I went along without mentioning it to Chris. On Saturday, while Michele, John and I were with Chris, in walked little David dressed in a colorful clown suit and cone shaped hat. Chris shook with laughter. I hadn't seen him enjoy a moment as much in many months. It turned out to be the right thing to do.

Because he was in a private room, I was not held to regular visiting hours. Once visitors had left and the nurse settled Chris for the night; then Christopher would want to talk. It was a continuation of what we had been doing all summer. At night, when there was no chance of interruption or that some-one would see him crying; then he felt free to verbally express his grief.

Each day, I mentally and emotionally tried to prepare myself for the heartbreak of listening to what Christopher was going to say. It was incredibly painful for him to share his deepest feel-ings; it was also agony for me to hear them. One night he said,

"All my dreams, all my dreams, my plans for the future are all gone. I can stand the pain, but I mind giving up my dreams." Another time, he said, "The only thing that matters is love. I just want to be with all of you." There was so much expressed in those two lines. I understood how separate he felt from all of us. It made me more determined than ever to be there for him in whatever way he needed me.

Dr. Martin came in to see Chris one morning, a week before Halloween. He told Chris that he did not believe there was any hope that he would survive this cancer. The embolization procedure had been unsuccessful. Chris was never going to walk again. Even with chemotherapy he would die within a few months. He suggested that Chris go home after the surgery to place the Hickman catheter in his chest was performed. They spoke for a long time. He told Chris that he would feel down and depressed, but he should not let it overwhelm him, and if he became depressed he should get counseling.

Chris thanked Dr. Martin and asked him to tell Maryann and me. We stood outside of Chris's room numb and sick to death as Dr. Martin repeated what he had told Chris; that there was no hope for his recovery and he only had a few months to live. I was finally hearing what I had dreaded hearing, but in my heart, I had already known. From that day eight months ago when Dr. Peters took Jack and me out into the hall and told us that Christopher probably had a hypernephroma; I knew that Chris was going to die. It was this reality, this knowledge that I had been struggling to suppress. And now Dr. Martin was telling us that that not only would he never walk again, but that his life would soon be over. Over before he had a chance to live! Chris would not recover. Christopher was going to die. We were going to lose him. We would have to bury our son. My son was going to die and leave us and all his dreams behind never to accomplish them. I would never see him again in this life. Gone were all his dreams and mine.

I wanted to scream and never stop. But how would that help

Chris? I needed to be strong, not fall apart. If I did, of what use would I be to Chris? It felt selfish to give in and simply let go. If he could endure his sentence, I would endure mine, if not for my sake, at least for his. He needed me to be strong and available all day long, and so I could not fall apart. Crying was all that I allowed myself. I couldn't help the tears. They simply fell many times a day without my ability to control them.

Dr. Martin said Chris had taken the news well. Knowing Chris that meant that he did not reveal his true anguish. Dr. Martin said that because we were a close knit family we would be able to handle it together. He suggested that we take Chris home. That was what Jack and I had longed to do for three weeks. In spite of the good care Chris was receiving, he was spending his life waiting for nurses, doctors, transportation, and meals. We hated when personnel forgot him in hallways or when an aid could not turn him properly. We were anxious to bring him home to the place he loved and had lived in since he was four years old.

In preparation for leaving the hospital, and so that Chris would be able to move from his bed to a wheel chair, Dr. Martin requested that Chris be fitted with a custom body brace to protect his fragile spine. Each day Chris was taken to rehab and taught how to get in and out of bed. One day I accompanied him so that I could learn how to help him when he came home.

During his stay in the hospital I had not seen him out of bed except for the times when two aides would transfer him from bed to a cart using a draw sheet. Now in rehab, I watched in horror as the nurse, after putting the back brace on, helped him to sit up and maneuver himself to the side of the bed, then on to a board. I was shocked to see how much Chris's condition had deteriorated in three weeks. He used his arms to slowly inch his way down the board to a wheel chair positioned next to the bed, and then struggled to get into the seat. His face was ashen, contorted with excruciating pain. I wanted to shout, "Stop this. Stop hurting him."

Chris turned his eyes toward me and a look passed between us that told me that once he was home he was not going to put himself through this ordeal. We both knew that the hospital was required to provide this training. But Chris and I knew with his spine so fragile, the pain escalating, and his abdomen increasingly edematous, by the time he came home, the body brace would not even fit. And without the brace he would not be able to move out of bed.

I accompanied Chris back to his room. We didn't have much to say. Chris was understandably quiet. My mind was reeling from the horror of seeing my once spirited son so incapacitated that he could not move three feet without incredible pain.

While we were sitting quietly, a young, pretty, blond candy stripper knocked and entered the room. She was probably a couple of years younger than Chris, and I like to think that in another time and place, perhaps they would have met – two young, attractive people on an equal footing. Instead, Chris was in a hospital bed, a morphine drip connected to his arm – a paraplegic in a hospital gown a world apart. How painful for Chris to have to experience feeling so helpless, and so removed from her young, vibrant, and healthy world.

With a bright smile, she greeted Chris and told him that she was from the rehab department, and was there to invite him on a week long camping and canoeing trip for paraplegics. Chris was ill at ease, but managed to listen politely, and then attempted to explain, "I don't think I can. You see, I have..."

But she interrupted and continued to cheerfully tell him of the many trip options available, and urged him to sign up. Again he tried, "I don't think that I..."

Again, she would not let him explain that, even though he was on the neurology floor with other paraplegics, he was not simply a paraplegic with a stable condition. He also had cancer, needed a hospital bed, and had to be connected to a morphine pump to endure the pain. It was obvious that she was simply following orders, and did not know or could not deal with knowing how sick Chris was. Finally, Chris stopped trying to explain and told her he would think about it.

I sat there speechless. I was still visualizing the incredible effort it had taken for him to simply move from the bed to the wheel chair. What kind of a super human effort would it take for him to endure sitting in a canoe for hours, and then suffer the hardship of camping out. It hurt that Chris had to endure this added affront.

When she left Chris looked at me, shook his head and said, "Maybe I should have told her that I only have a week to live, so I can only go on a three day trip." It was so macabre that we laughed hysterically – until the tears came. Then we cried uncontrollably because reality hurt so much. The truth of his condition had been brought home so cruelly.

Our experience at the University Hospital had been devastating. It had been one long three week agony during which we had gone from hope to despair that Chris could be cured. If not to be cured, at least to have a chance at a cure, one small window of hope. But no! Dr. Martin said, "There is no hope. I have had a lot of experience with hyernephromas." Jack said that he sounded like Father Marin in the Exorcist who had had many dealings with the devil. This was our devil and we were being told that the devil was too strong and Chris would not make it.

When we learned that nothing more could be done for Chris, Jack and I spoke with Doctor Martin and told him we wanted to take care of Chris at home. He encouraged us to do so. He said that we could get nursing help, perhaps through Hospice. He assured us that he and Dr. Paul would provide medical assistance by phone while local physicians could become part of the medical team and provide hands-on care. There had never been any doubt in Jack's mind or my mine that we wanted to care for Chris at home, now it was a matter of working out the details.

It would be necessary to have nursing care because Chris, paralyzed from his chest to his toes, would need to be turned every three to four hours or his circulation would be impaired and skin ulcers would develop. I could not lift and turn him without the help of another person. He had lost bowel control, and would need someone to clean and bathe him and replace the chux. At that point, I was hesitant both for myself and for Chris to do this for him. However, later, as Chris became sicker, he wanted Jack or me instead of the nurse to do as much for him as we could, and cleaning him and changing the chux were no longer a point of embarrassment for either Chris or me.

Having nursing care would mean that I could leave the house each morning to go to Mass and grocery shop. Daily Mass had always been a source of comfort and renewal. If I could begin each day with prayer and meditation, then I would have the strength and the ability to focus on Chris for the rest of the day.

When Jack and I told Chris that we wanted him to come home, he hesitated and questioned if we could care for him in his condition. He wanted to come home, but he was worried that it would be too much for us and not sure that we were up to the task. We assured him that we wanted him to be home, and could take care of him. There would be nurses around the clock so it would not be too much work for me. Instead of being upstairs in his room, the family room would be set up for him. Some furniture would be removed, so that we could bring in a hospital bed and any equipment that he would need. This would be a better arrangement, because he would not be isolated upstairs, and we could be together as a family. We explained that even though we would have twenty-four hour a day nursing care, the nurse did not have to sit in the room with him. She could sit in the living room; when he needed her he could call her. I told him he would be in charge.

He was relieved and happy to be coming home knowing that we wanted to take care of him and that it could work. I knew I could take care of Chris, and I really wanted to. The awful week before Chris went into the hospital had taught me to be more resourceful and patient. Now I felt empowered.

When we met with Dr. Martin, we asked if Chris could

receive not only chemo, but also morphine through the Hickman catheter that was soon to be placed in his chest? If it were possible, then Chris would not have to have morphine injections, or receive morphine through a catheter in his arm, or resort to other types of pain killers like the Brompton cocktail. This would give him the greatest relief from pain.

Dr. Martin sent in Beth, the home care liaison nurse, who believed there might be a way that morphine could be delivered through the Hickman catheter instead of through a catheter in the arm, because providentially, such a device had become available in the last two months. The next day, Willie, the pharmacist from a medical supply house that furnishes medications and intravenous fluids to patients in their homes, explained that a new computerized device that used cartridges of morphine had become available. The cartridge and computer could be connected to the Hickman catheter through a tube. If a double lumen type of Hickman were installed into the subclavian vein in Chris's chest, it would mean that Chris could receive morphine through one port and chemotherapy through the second port. It was a great relief to know that this state of the art devise existed. Chris would be the first patient going home from the University Center with such a device.

At last we were receiving some good news. Chris readily agreed to this method for receiving morphine and after discussing it with the family, he requested that Dr. Martin schedule the surgery to place the Hickman Catheter with the double lumen.

The morning of the surgery I arrived in Chris's room to find him close to tears. He had been informed that before surgery he would have to go for radiation therapy and physical therapy. Chris knew from experience that if he tried to go to radiation and physical therapy he would not be back in time for surgery. Consequently, he had asked them to change the times for radiation and physical therapy. But the nurse insisted he would be able to do all three without any changes. He was overwhelmed by his inability to get the staff to understand, and he was afraid surgery would need to be rescheduled. He was beside himself with frustration and helplessness. I remember bolting from his room ready to start shouting. I understood Shirley McLain's frustration in "Terms of Endearment" when she barged out of her daughter's room and screamed at the nurses at the nursing station. I was about to do the same thing. Fortunately, Dr. Martin was walking into the room as I was storming out of it. I explained that Chris was scheduled to do three things within an hour's time, and that included surgery, and he kindly dealt with rescheduling rehab and radiation therapy.

Christopher was taken down to surgery but it did not go smoothly. He said it was a fiasco. He had to remind them that he had not signed a surgical release form allowing them to perform surgery. Surgery was delayed while they waited for the release form. Next, Chris asked whether the surgeon knew he would be placing the catheter with the double lumen instead of the one with the single port. It was fortunate that he checked, because no one was aware that he was supposed to have a double lumen. Surgery was again delayed while the correct catheter was sent for. Finally, the surgeon Chris was supposed to have, the expert in placing the Hickman catheter, was now on vacation. Another surgeon performed the surgery. Instead of taking a half-hour, the surgery took an hour and a half. Throughout the surgery the physician showed his frustration.

The next morning, when Beth examined the site of the Hickman, she expressed dismay that a stitch had not been placed at the site where the Hickman tubing went into the skin. I surmised that the surgeon who had done the surgery had little experience placing the Hickman. I was heartsick because there had been another debacle. Beth examined and cleansed the area, then applied another clear plastic bandage over the site and stated it seemed to be okay. We hoped for the best. In a couple of weeks we were to sorely regret that Chris had not had a more experienced surgeon.

Christopher spent the next few days getting used to the

Hickman. He began receiving chemotherapy and morphine continuously, each from a separate port. The morphine cartridge was inserted into a small device or pump the size of a small cell phone and controlled by means of a built-in computer. A clear narrow plastic tube delivered the morphine from the cartridge to the port inserted into the subclavean vein in Chris's chest. If he experienced a sharp pain he was able to give himself a bolus dose, an immediate dose of morphine.

When Chris came home from the hospital his morphine needs were 4 milligrams an hour. On the night he died seven and one-half months later, his dosage was 92 milligrams an hour. Yet he never used more than he needed to alleviate the pain. His need increased because of the spread of the malignancy; and over time the pain receptors in his body built up a tolerance to the morphine and so he needed more to control the pain.

After the surgery, Willie the pharmacist came in and explained the pump to Chris. Chris, a natural in understanding things mechanical, was able to grasp the concept immediately. Within an hour, he understood how it worked, how it was to be cleaned, how it could be programmed for continuous flow, how to give himself a bolus dose, and how to change the morphine cartridge. At home he was going to be able to take care of the whole thing himself. It was the psychological lift he needed. It boosted his self confidence and put him in touch with the creative and self-sufficient part of himself that had been dormant since his arrival at the hospital.

I too learned how to take care of the pump. Chris taught me because he knew that some day he would be unable to take care of it himself. I took care of the pump only once, on the night he died, because for the first time, he was unable to do it himself. I will always be grateful to Steri-Pharm for the morphine pump because it controlled Chris's pain to the extent that Chris was able to relate to all of us as he always had, and he was able to maintain quality relationships until a few days before he died. That was of paramount importance to Chris and to those of us who loved him.

After his surgery his spirits lifted. He seemed to take heart because he was now receiving chemotherapy. And he was happy that he would soon be going home. Jack and I too felt relieved that something positive was being done for him. Despite there being no hope, we clung to hope. We prayed as we had throughout the many, many months of Christopher's cancer that a miracle would cure him. We clung to the hope that the chemotherapy would stop the cancer.

Now we were eager to bring Chris home. We had no doubt that we could take good care of him. While I was in Milwaukee with Chris, Jack and I worked out the steps we had to take before we could bring Chris home. Working in different cities, the two of us implemented our plan, arranging for Steri-Pharm to provide morphine cartridges and most of the other pharmaceuticals and supplies that Chris would need when he came home. We made arrangements to have nursing care around the clock, and Jack had the family room, now Chris's room, cleaned from top to bottom. Most of the furniture was removed and a hospital bed was brought in.

Despite the knowledge that we were bringing Chris home without hope of him recovering, we were feeling very positive. During those three weeks at the hospital, I had walked through the halls feeling defeated and depressed. I hated what Chris had endured while he was there. I hated knowing the truth of his condition. I wanted to take Chris home and never return.

Now, it was good to take action so that Chris and I could return to the warmth and comfort of home, to the place he loved. I was anxious to take care of him myself, to serve him his favorite foods, to be with him. I continued to pray for his complete recovery. But if it were not to be, then I wanted Chris at home where I could be with him during this, the last and most important part of his short life.

⚜ 7 ⚜

CHRIS COMES HOME – A TIME OF SOUL-MAKING

The sight of the empty hospital bed in our family room ready to receive our son was a shock. Even though I knew what Jack had done to prepare for Chris's arrival, I was not prepared for the change. The transformation of this room was a symbol of how much our life had changed. The carefree days were gone. Tearfully I looked around at the room where much of our life had taken place for over twenty years. It's where we watched television, where homework was done, snacks were eaten, bills were paid, games were played, and hobbies enjoyed. It's where I mended, knitted, and read. Communion, confirmation, birthday parties -our family's life had taken place in this room. Our family had grown up in this room. And now it was going to have another important role as it became a hospital room, Chris's room. The phase we were about to enter was going to test our humanity. It was going to be a time of soul-making.

With heavy hearts we continued to transform the room as we emptied the sweater chest from Chris's bedroom and brought it into the family room. Now it would hold hospital sheets, towels, and medical supplies. We set the television and VCR on top of it. A small chest for toiletries was placed on the hearth behind Chris's bed for easy access. The desk surface would become the nurse's station. A half-bath off the kitchen was equipped with antiseptic soap, wash basin, and other necessary items.

Jack and I had left the hospital the evening before, October 28th, so that I could do the last minute things that would need to be done before Chris's arrival the following morning. Maryann had arranged for time away from her hospital responsibilities so that she could stay with Chris that morning, and accompany him to the ambulance that would bring him home.

I had learned months before that I could still function despite sadness and depression. That morning, I set about making chicken soup and a pie, in the hope that the house would smell like home when Chris arrived at noon. We had been away from home for almost a month, and Chris had been eating hospital food exclusively. Now I was eager to feed and nurture him.

At eleven, the nursing supervisor, arrived with several nurses and set up the desk as a nurse's station and made sure that all of the necessary supplies were on hand. I had the opportunity to explain to Marsha that, although we needed to have a nurse available twenty-four hours a day, it would not be a physically taxing assignment. Since we wanted to maintain our privacy and our family relationships as much as possible, I asked that the nurse on duty sit in the living room where she would be free to read, knit, or write letters until Chris called her. Marsha understood and would convey our request to her nurses.

Around Noon, on a cool, sunny day, the ambulance pulled into our driveway. The trip from Wisconsin to Michigan City provided Chris with his last glimpse of colorful fall foliage. It was to be the last time that Chris would be outdoors. Jack helped the ambulance attendants bring Chris into the family room and into his bed, the bed he would live in until May 5th, almost seven months later.

Despite the circumstances, it was so good to have Chris home and to be home myself. I had spent three weeks practically living at the hospital, going to Maryann and Dave's home only to sleep. Now, despite the grief, I felt energetic and grateful for the opportunity to take care of Chris at home. We were fortunate that Chris was not confined to a room in a hospital for this important part of his life. We wanted him to live in the room he loved since he was four.

It was a warm, comfortable room with a beamed ceiling, and a brick fireplace and hearth across one wall. Warm walnut paneling covered the walls and two almost floor to ceiling windows looked out over a small courtyard and to the street beyond. At first, Chris didn't want the drapes opened more than a crack because he wanted to maintain his privacy. We had a lot of walkers in our small neighborhood of one hundred and ten homes. Many of them knew of Chris's illness and homecoming. If the drapes were fully opened Chris, the hospital bed, and the trapeze over his bed would be visible. He couldn't bear being seen as a paraplegic. However, he always wanted the windows open so that he could smell the outdoors. After a few days, we were able to partially open the drapes so that he could look out but not be seen by anyone taking a walk.

Since the family room was adjacent to the entryway and next to the kitchen, there were two entries into the family room and no real privacy. Within a couple of days, it became apparent that unless we made some rules, Chris would have no privacy. Chris requested that we ask friends to refrain from simply dropping in.

Since Chris was paralyzed from his chest down to his toes, he needed help with everything. At first he could manage with a urinal; but soon, because of bladder infections common with paraplegics, he had to have a permanent catheter. He could not sit on a bedpan, so he had to have large disposable liners under him. Because of the paralysis he had no bowel or bladder control, a condition that caused him great distress and embarrassment. Although visitors would have understood, he would have been terribly embarrassed if he lost control while a visitor was there.

He was reluctant to allow a steady stream of visitors; consequently visits from extended family and friends were very limited. Jack and I didn't mind because we knew how difficult his life was, and we knew what a tremendous effort he was making to accept his circumstances. His inability to walk and the loss of his bodily functions were his greatest crosses. He said, "Having cancer wouldn't be so bad if I could walk and take care of myself, and still drive to the lake to watch the sunset." The sorrow and longing that I saw on his face broke my heart.

The first few days were spent adjusting to our new situation, to accepting the sight of Chris paralyzed and in a hospital bed in our family room, to having a nurse in our home around the clock. It was devastating for all of us. While Chris was still in the hospital, he had said, "Mom, I don't want you to get exhausted taking care of me. I want you to let the nurses do as much as possible. Let them do the work. I don't want you or Dad coming down at night. The nurse on duty can help me." I told him that we would go along with whatever he wanted. He was in charge. He could tell his Dad, the nurse, or me what he wanted us to do for him.

There were so many aspects of his life over which he had no control. I wanted to insure that whenever possible he made the decisions. He was in charge and in control. I told him that he would decide when he wanted to sit up, when and what he wanted to eat, when he wanted to be turned, and who could visit him. He could call the nurse or tell me to call her. He had so few freedoms, that I wanted to make sure no one usurped the ones he had. My role, as I saw it, was to support Chris in his decisions. In our home, the only thing that would be done strictly by the book would be his medical care: medications, temperature, and IV's when needed. The rest, his meals, bath, linen changes, bedtime, visitors, would be according to Chris's wishes. I wanted his life to be as unregimented as possible given his circumstance.

We were relieved to be home again. Life was settling into a routine. Chris was feeling well enough that he could try to forget about the fact that he was in bed and had cancer. As soon as he was through with his morning routine, he would call me in to keep him company. I'd move the desk chair close to his bed so that we could talk quietly or watch TV together, and I spent most of the day there. We talked, shared a lot of things that were going on in Maryann's, Michele's, and John's lives. Maryann was pregnant again and due in January. Soon Dave would be finished with his training and they were considering coming to Michigan City to open a practice. Michele was doing well in her job and had been transferred to a small Chicago sub-urb that reminded her of Michigan City. John would be driving in again on the weekend as he did every weekend in order to be with Chris. We watched "This Old House" and talked at length about building construction, Chicago architecture, and real estate - subjects that we both loved. In retrospect those first weeks seemed almost idyllic compared to the last few weeks.

Journal Entry • November 4, 1986

So much has happened in nine months, and I haven't been able to write. All has been internalized and then spoken to the Lord. Our lives are so changed, changed forever. Chris is home from Milwaukee. Three weeks of tests and a trip to the Medical Center in Madison for a new procedure – emolization. Nothing could be done for him. He is a paraplegic now and lives in a hospital bed in our family room – the room he played in since he was four years old. We are all changed – we've been on a long journey through pain, fear, hope, terror, tears, love, despair, and we are still in process. I emerge no longer caring about so many things – the props of my life. I have been washed by Chris's suffering and mine, by his hopes and mine, by his love for me and mine for him.

We have prayed, cried, hoped, and feared together. We have become symbiotic. I am most content when I am near Chris and can see and hear him. He too wants me around – never too far away. When company or the kids are coming, Chris says, "You'll be here won't you, Mom?" He worries about us. He said, "I just want to be with you guys." I translate it as meaning he doesn't want to die and leave us. Those words have cut into my heart and brain! They say it all!

I'm changed. Life has new and different meaning now. Each day I want to thank the Holy Trinity for today, for my children, for their health, for Jack, for family and friends. I especially want to thank God for Chris being with us today, for his being able to speak to us. Today he is able to share his thoughts with us. He can eat and laugh with us. I must be aware of each day's grace and gifts because tomorrow one of the gifts may be gone, so I must appreciate them today.

We take the ability to walk, to shower, to control our bowel and bladder functions for granted. The ability to stand and walk, to care for one's own needs, to be pain-free are gifts, not prerogatives. These are truly the gifts of life – all the rest are nice, but they are unnecessary and useless in the final analysis.

Chris is gentle and considerate of his nurses. He doesn't complain or criticize; yet he is in pain. He does criticize Jack and me and gets impatient with us. But I understand. We are the only ones over whom he can exercise some control, maybe because we love him so much.

Yesterday afternoon, his fraternity brothers from Purdue, Mark (Flash as Chris calls him) and Eric came for two hours. They brought a video that they had made for Chris showing the fraternity house, the brothers, and scenes from Purdue. They asked many of Chris's friends and acquaintances to talk to him on the video. Chris loved it. They all laughed a lot as they brought him up to date on life at Purdue. Chris had a wonderful time with them. In the kitchen Mark asked me if he could come again. I said yes as long as Chris was up to a visit. He asked how Chris was doing. I told him he needs a miracle. Mark simply put his arm around me and gave me a hug.

Hundreds of images of Chris at various stages of his life pass through my mind. I think about all his talents: his great mind, his love of photography and carpentry, railroading, gardening, landscaping. I see him driving our boat. I see Chris the intellectual. Chris, my beloved son and friend. I'm crying again. An hour ago I was drained and tearless.

I hated the last few days at the University hospital even though it was a beautiful structure with a hotel-like lobby and gorgeous views of the brilliant colors of fall. It was a place of pain, disap-

pointment, and lost hope of Chris recovering. After nine months, we had to be in Milwaukee to hear that there was no medical hope for him. But oh! I do hope and pray and have faith in Jesus that he will send the Holy Spirit to breathe new life in his spine and legs and heal his cancerous spreads. I believe if I do all that I can, Jesus will do all that He is able to do. Jesus can do anything and every-thing — the lame walk, the blind see, the deaf hear. I am more impressed than ever by Jesus' miracles. To heal a spinal cord so that it can respond to the brain's messages again is truly incredible, impossible for medicine to do. How great is your power, oh Lord!

During the first days that Chris was home, I simply watched as the nurses worked, changed sheets, placed draw sheets, and lifted Chris. I began to realize that the nurses were not equally competent. Some could lift him better than others. Some placed the draw sheet in such a way that it did not ride up dur-ing the next turn. Some were more flexible than others while some needed the regimentation of a hospital and didn't func-tion well in a home setting. Some needed to be totally in charge. Some walked and spoke softly while others talked loud-ly. One nurse wanted to convert him to fundamentalism. Most of them wanted him to be happy. They wanted him to laugh and joke with them. They wanted to mother him, to nurse him back to health, to heal him. The ones who were mothers had the hardest time of all. He broke their hearts. Unfortunately, he wasn't able to satisfy their needs.

During the course of those seven months there were over twenty nurses who cared for Christopher. A few of them were there on a regular basis from one to three times a week for eight-hour periods. Temporaries who had free time and who wanted to earn extra money filled in the rest of the shifts.

Of all of the nurses the two with whom Chris had the best relationships were Debbie and Sherry. Debbie was a young mother who, unbeknownst to us until shortly before Chris died, had lost her five-year-old son, a year and a half before.

Sherry had nursed her husband through bone cancer just as we were doing. Neither of these women told Chris of their own losses. They simply conveyed positive regard, compassion, and competence and he responded to them. He didn't feel any pressure from them to be anything other than who he was. They didn't expect him to chat with them if he was not in the mood, and he didn't disappointment them when he was not feeling cheerful. They didn't judge him or his mood. They understood that he was in the process of letting go of everything and everyone that he loved and he had neither energy nor desire to make new friends. These two nurses were efficient, kind, and helpful without being overbearing. They met his needs; they didn't expect him to fulfill theirs.

Vicki was another nurse whom we considered to be special. Chris said, "I don't understand why she always says, 'Thank you, Chris.' whenever I ask her to do something for me." He never asked her why she thanked him, but he expressed wonder to me. After his death she confided that she had always thanked Chris whenever he asked for her help because she understood how difficult it was for him to relinquish any more of his independence.

Because he was a paraplegic, he needed to change his position every two to three hours or his circulation would be impaired and skin ulcers would develop. For the first two or three weeks, it was possible for the nurse alone to help Chris to turn to a different position. However, within a couple of weeks, as his condition deteriorated and as we realized that some nurses were not as adept as others in turning him, Jack or I helped the nurse to turn him.

Despite all our precautions, Chris did eventually develop skin ulcers on both hips. Thankfully our friend and gifted surgeon, Dr. Rade Pejic provided the care Chris needed. Each Sunday morning, after making rounds on his hospital patients, Rade came to our home and debreeded and dressed Chris's ulcers. We will forever be grateful for his help.

Another problem soon arose because all of the nurses wore

their own favorite cologne. Chris complained to me that as
they lifted him or bent over him their scents nauseated him.
He asked me to request that they refrain from using scents.
All but one or two of the nurses honored that request. When
anyone did come in wearing cologne, we tried hard to do without her help. If Jack was at home, he and I turned him.

I watched the nurses and became aware that their abilities
varied depending on their training and experience. I also listened when Chris told me which nurses couldn't lift him without jerking the draw sheet and causing him great pain, and
which nurses could change the sheets smoothly. I began to
realize that his treatment had to be standardized if his pain
were to be kept to a minimum. This was particularly important
because of the number of nurses needed to cover the twenty-
one shifts each week.

Another factor responsible for Chris's increased pain was
his condition – it was unstable and changed from day to day.
What worked today might not work tomorrow. He had fevers
that were caused by the cancer; but some of them were the
result of bladder infections and the presence of the Hickman
catheter. The tumor in Chris's spinal canal continued to erode
the surrounding bone causing painful fractures along his spine
and more loss of feeling in his chest. In addition there was
metastasis of the cancer to the lymphatic system resulting in
fluid retention in his abdomen and lower limbs. Consequently
he was getting heavier and harder to lift. Therefore, Chris had
to be turned very carefully due to the tumor in his spinal canal
and to the fragile condition of his spine.

After lifting him with the draw sheet and bringing him to one
side of the bed, he needed to be rolled on his side and pillows
had to be propped behind him, in front of him, and between
his knees so that his body was fully supported. Six pillows were
positioned every time he turned. As his pain increased or shift-
ed, the pillow positions changed. If Jack wasn't at home, the
nurse and I lifted him. If a new nurse was on duty, I explained

each step before we started the lift to avoid painful mistakes. If a nurse had not been on duty for a week or two, I brought her up-to-date on the changes in his condition. If a nurse was on duty that we knew from past experience could not lift Chris smoothly, Jack came home for a few minutes to assist me with the lift; because if the lift was not smooth, Christopher sustained tremendous pain. A careless, jerky movement caused hours of increased pain. One time the fine, clear tubing coming from the Hickman site beneath the clavical became wrapped up in the top sheet. The nurse carelessly gave a yank to straighten the sheet and jerked the tubing, loosening it at the site, causing Chris excruciating pain. Experiences like that made us very cautious in the way we cared for Chris. It relieved Chris's apprehension when Jack and I lifted him. Then too, the sicker he became the more he wanted us, his mom and dad, to be personally involved in caring for him.

The draw sheet and the disposable chux were a constant source of trouble. As Chris turned from side to side, the chux would ride up. The draw sheet too had a tendency to ride up, making it useless as a sheet protector and as an aid in lifting him. Chris and I spent many hours discussing ways to prevent this from happening and finally succeeded. They were small but important victories because as Chris's condition worsened and the pain in his back increased, he couldn't tolerate sheet and draw sheet changes every day. Consequently it was extremely important to have the chux remain in the proper place so that Chris did not have to endure rolling over two sets of sheets as the old sheets were removed and the fresh ones put in place. Since there were only three nurses who were able to correctly place the draw sheet so that it wouldn't ride up quickly, I took over the responsibility of changing the bottom sheet and placing the draw sheet.

Each week the medical supply house called and we placed an order for whatever supplies were needed including the morphine cartridges that supplied the pump attached to the Hickman catheter. During the first couple of weeks, whenever Steri-Pharm called to ask what supplies were needed, the nurse on duty would check supplies and place the order. However, after several orders were placed incorrectly and Chris almost ran out of morphine a couple of times, we realized that the order needed to be placed by someone who was there every day and knew how quickly supplies were being used. If the nurse on duty was one of the ones that came several times a week and was familiar with Chris's changing needs, then she placed the order. If a new nurse was on duty when the supply house called, then Jack or Chris and I placed the order because we knew what supplies were rapidly diminishing.

When Chris came home from the hospital in late October he was running a low-grade fever. Since the nurse was taking his temperature at least once during every shift, it was easy to monitor how often Chris had a fever. His oncologist in Milwaukee thought that the fevers were due to the cancer. Aspirin seemed to help to control the fevers however, by the second week in November the fevers increased. They were not high all the time, but sometimes they reached 101 and 102 degrees. We began to be concerned that something else was going on. Several antibiotics were tried with no result. A urine culture indicated there was no bacterium in the urine. Beth, our home health care liaison from Milwaukee suggested the infection might be at the sight of the Hickman catheter. A blood sample would need to be taken in order to identify the bacteria so that the appropriate antibiotic could be prescribed. Since Chris could not leave his bed, a lab technician from the medical laboratory came to our home to draw Chris's blood, but it would take two days to grow the culture and get the result.

In the meantime, Chris's fever shot up to 104 degrees. His whole body shook uncontrollably. He said he was freezing cold and asked for a woolen cap to cover his head. Aspirin and the antibiotic he was taking were not effective. For two days, the nurse on duty and Jack and I worked almost around the clock trying to bring the fever down with cool soaks on his head, underarms, and chest. Five minutes after placing the cool towel on his body it was hot and needed to be changed again. John, Michele and Maryann and Dave waited anxiously for the culture result as did Jack and I. All of us were terrified that Chris would die from the infection.

Finally and thankfully, the bacterium was isolated and an antibiotic was prescribed. But it would have to be given intravenously. Christopher insisted that the antibiotic be given through one of the ports in the Hickman catheter rather than by way of an intravenous needle in his arm. This would mean that one of the ports, either the one through which he was receiving the morphine or the one through which he was receiving the chemo, would have to be used for the antibiotic. The result would be that either the morphine or the chemo would have to be discontinued at least for the time during which he would be on the antibiotic. Chris said that he wanted to have the IV with the antibiotic go into the port that was providing the chemotherapy. I knew that he thought it was no use anyway. Much to our sadness, the chemotherapy was discontinued and he started receiving the antibiotic through the Hickman catheter.

A week and a half later, he was still receiving the antibiotic through the port in the Hickman and not receiving chemotherapy. But at least the antibiotic was working because the bacteria had been isolated and correctly identified. We called Beth to tell her that the bacteria had been identified as staph aureus, coagulase positive, also known as "golden death." It is the type that is acquired most frequently in hospitals. She was very familiar with it. Immediately I thought of the surgery to place the Hickman catheter. Had he acquired it then? We would never know.

Finally the fever came down to a low-grade fever that could be attributed to the cancer. When finally the IV was discontinued, I asked Christopher if he was ready to go back on chemotherapy.

He said he didn't want to go back on it right now. He would tell us when he was ready. He never did go back on chemo. He told me months later that he had expected to die quickly after he came home from the hospital and developed the staph aureus infection. He felt there was no point in resuming chemotheraphy. If he had not had that hospital borne infection, I feel certain that he would have continued with the chemotherapy. Because of the infection Chris had lost even the small hope that chemotherapy could help him to recover. Could the chemo have been the miracle that would have kept him alive and for which we had been storming heaven?

During the time that he had the high fever and cold soaks were being applied to his forehead, Chris would bring the cloth down over his eyes. He continued to bring the cloth down over his eyes for about a week. He seemed to want the cloth over his eyes a lot more than perhaps he would have needed it. I believe he created and withdrew into a personal space where he privately worked through the painful awareness that he was going to die. I believe during that time that he dealt with his broken heart, the loss of his dreams, the loss of his future, and the loss of his loved ones. I'm sure, because I know Chris, that he did a lot of thinking during those days when he had the cloth over his eyes. During that time I believe that he came to the realization that the ordeal was going to get worse; he was facing an agony of unbelievable proportions. I believe that he decided to completely give up on chemotherapy during that time. I'm sure he cried quietly to himself as he let go of his hopes for the future. When he finally took the cloth away from his eyes after those feverish days were over, he did so because he had accepted what was happening to him and he was ready to deal with it on another level.

Journal Entry • December 1, 1986

Each day I see Chris getting sicker. My heart feels like an open wound, as though it is going through a shredder and I'm bleeding internally. Yesterday and today he lost control of his bladder function. Another blow, another loss of control. He feels such pain when he has to turn. It becomes unbearable when the draw sheet needs to be changed. Having a capable nurse on duty when the draw sheet needs changing becomes crucial; Shari is the best. How he suffers when he must roll over the new and old draw sheets. I suffer with him, and yet I can't feel the actual pain; and so I am separated from him in this. I suffer mental and emotional anguish, but I can't truly know the pain. In that, he is all alone. My son, alone!

I can't follow him into eternity or be there to greet him when he gets there, as I had done when he came home from school. There'll be no greeting from me. But I think that my grandmother will be there for him, as will other family members. And most of all, the Lord God will be there to meet him.

The spiritual world is now more real to me than this world. I am so aware of my grandmother. It is as though she is imparting her strength to me to endure, to love, to give without reproach or anger. This is not me! It is prayer and love, and the love and prayers of our family and friends (known and unknown) that are helping us to get through.

Chris, my joy, is remarkable. How he suffers. Yet he has such quiet strength. My heart breaks! I look at his beautiful face, so thin and childlike, but still handsome with dark, good looks. His hair is over his ears and dirty; but it doesn't smell bad somehow. He has a beard. He only has strength to shave once a week. He tries to stagger these jobs. He thinks things out so quietly and carefully. He takes full charge of his Hickman catheter – cleaning it, changing the tubing and cartridges. He figures out the morphine doses with Steri-Pharm's help. If anything, he is frugal with the doses, rather than generous. Sometimes, when I have seen that his pain has increased, I've suggested that he increase the dose, or give himself a bolus dose. But he is in charge of this. He is glad that he can at least be in charge of this. He has so little control over other aspects of his life. He complains about not having control. But when we talk at night, I've told him that he has control over how he chooses to react to things that happen during the day. He chooses how he interacts with each of us. It helps him to know this.

He wants to write letters but he never does, or doesn't have the energy. My son, my joy, my friend. How I will miss him! What will I be like afterwards? People ask how I'm doing. I sometimes say, "Ok," at other times I say, "I don't know, I've never done this before, so I don't know how I'm doing!"

It breaks my heart to enter Chris's bedroom upstairs. All his things, his possessions are there – his clothes, his shoes. They reflect his spirit, likes, hobbies, and interests, HIS ROOM.

I die each time I imagine life without Chris, my friend. What a waste! What talent! What a mind! What a lover of life! I will always remember, "Mom, I just want to be with you guys!"

Journal Entry • December 4, 1986

Chris's temperature only rose to 100 degrees during the night – a real break! He is on a Foley catheter now. There is a good chance that he will have more bladder infections now because he is on the Foley, but he has no control over his bladder sphincter so he must be on a catheter. Maybe he'll regain control again after the E. Coli infection clears up.

I went to the grocery store as usual yesterday. I search the isles looking for some kind of treat for Chris – something to increase the appeal of food for him. I'm so conscious of doing these things for him for the last time. Am I buying Mint Milano cookies for him for the last time? I rack my brain for foods to make which he enjoyed in the past and may be having for the last time.

In spite of all the infections and changes in Chris's condition, our life settled into a familiar pattern. Chris, Jack, and I had little rituals that helped us to cope. After Chris's 6:00 a.m. turn, he would go back to sleep; but I would quickly shower, dress, and go to the 7:00 a.m. Mass, pick up groceries or maybe make a quick stop for coffee. When I returned Chris would be ready to sit up. I'd open the drapes, and remove the intercom that he used during the night to call me; meanwhile the nurse took his temperature and set out his medications. I'd sit next to Chris as he decided what to have for breakfast and afterwards we'd visit until he was ready to care for the Hickman catheter, bathe and shave. We'd continue to sit together talking until 11 a.m. when it was necessary for him to turn on his side. Chris would nap off and on and I would move from the chair next to his bed to the lounge chair and read or leave for an hour to do errands.

After the nurse and I lifted him back to a sitting position, I'd serve Chris his lunch and sit next to him, and we'd spend the afternoon together sometimes watching a program or two on television. Chris seemed to enjoy "Leave It To Beaver." It reminded him of an earlier carefree time and of his relationship with his own brother. When Jack came home from the office, he'd join us in the family room and Chris would say, "Dad, get comfortable. Take off your tie and shoes and relax."

Jack, who was "out in the world" shared the news of the day; then Chris and I shared our day with Jack – observations, insights, messages from friends. Often we needed to update him on Chris's medical needs, a new pain and what it might mean, prescriptions that needed to be refilled, calls which would have to be made to one of his doctors.

We were working together to solve problems. The three of us became a team. We were doing this together and as we nurtured one another, we drew strength. Through it all, we were aware of our own and each other's pain and impending loss. The future colored each day making it precious. Today and a few tomorrows were all we had together. They were not perfect days, but they were better than tomorrow. We were learning to see and appreciate the gifts present in each day.

After dinner, there were usually one or two phone calls from Chris's friends and from Michele, Maryann, or John. We'd leave the room so that Chris could have privacy to talk; but we remained nearby because Chris always wanted us to join him as soon as he was finished with his calls. When friends called, he tried to make his voice sound strong as it had when he was well. He was still being asked for advice and input especially from his fraternity brothers. When he hung up the phone, his voice would return to the weak, soft pitch that was the result of the paralysis which impeded his lungs from fully expanding.

We'd remain with Chris all evening – talking, watching television, and solving problems. The nurse would come in to dispense Chris's medication, check IVs when he was on them, or to give him a morphine cartridge when he needed to replace the empty one. Then she would return to the living room.

The three of us were more energized and upbeat on Friday, knowing that John would come home on Saturday to be with Chris. Once a month, Maryann, Dave, and little David would come from Milwaukee, arriving late Friday night and leaving on Sunday. Michele came less frequently, but she called Chris several times a week. She lived two and one-half hours away, but more than that she had a very difficult time seeing Chris's deteriorating condition. Chris knew what she was going through and told me that he worried about how she would handle his death.

Since Jack, John, and Chris enjoyed Saturday television sports, it was my chance to leave for a couple of hours to renew myself. On the weekends I had more energy and more free time to spend cooking and baking. It was good to concentrate on normal activities. Even on weekends when there were more of us, we simply set up more TV trays, brought in extra chairs and ate with Christopher. We were learning that love means supporting each other and drawing strength from being together. Amazingly we even managed to laugh a lot as we watched one year old David and his antics. I loved to see Chris's spirit visibly brightened as he watched David walk and talk. But beneath the surface we grieved knowing that even this would not last forever. Soon Chris would leave us and we would have to continue without his physical presence in our lives.

Sunday afternoons our spirits would sink because everyone had to leave. It sharply pointed out the difference between Chris and his brother and sisters. They were healthy and could leave to resume their busy lives. Chris could go nowhere. There was no fulfilling life to resume, his bed, his room was all there was. Sunday nights were sad and quiet as we each reflected on our depressing situation. Chris would become irritable and critical complaining about the nurses and little things that he usually ignored.

Thanksgiving and Christmas were a mixed blessing. But we were together and grateful for that gift. We performed the external rituals; we had turkey and dressing with all the trimmings and pumpkin pie. But there was no inner joy for any of us. We were all in pain as we remembered how carefree we had been and with what enthusiasm we had celebrated the holidays in the past. There always had been extended family to help us celebrate. This year we had discouraged our family from coming to be with us. This time was for us. We wanted to be alone with just our immediate family. As we gathered together in the family room to say grace before having dinner, we were terribly conscious that this was the last Thanksgiving and Christmas that we would have with Christopher.

Before Christmas Chris and I discussed whether we should put up a tree. Chris didn't want one and Jack and I had no heart for one either. Several friends sent large pots of poinsettias and these I placed in the living room where Chris could see them from his bed. Chris chose the menu and I baked a few of our favorite cookies and a pie and served our favorite Christmas dinner.

We had always made a grand production of exchanging and opening presents. But this year, exchanging material Christmas presents seemed inappropriate to all of us and we decided not to. Chris didn't want any and we understood. The only gift we wanted was Chris's recovery and only God could give us that gift. I ended up buying some toys for little David and we watched and laughed as he played with them.

During the Christmas season without our knowledge Maryann and David ordered a chalice and ciborium inscribed with Chris's name from a Catholic missionary order that provides religious articles to missionaries in need of them. The chalice and ciborium would be sent to a missionary who would use them in the celebration of the mass while also remembering his benefactor, Chris, in his prayers. But before they would be sent to the missions Maryann and David wanted them to be used for Chris's funeral Mass. Shortly before Chris died Maryann and Dave told us about the gift they had purchased in Christopher's memory and their desire that they be used at Chris's Mass.

Chris's twenty-third birthday, New Year's Eve, was another devastating day. John came home to be with Chris, to share his last birthday. Maryann was in her eighth month and would not be able to come. Michele would also not be there because of the great emotional toll it would take. I asked Chris if I could make a birthday cake for him but he didn't want the usual birthday cake with candles. He didn't want to be reminded of the significance of 23 candles knowing there would never be 24 candles. I suggested that we have a pie. He thought that an ice cream pie would be good. We had no material gifts for him. Maryann and Michele had sent him cards and John, Jack, and I also gave him cards in which we expressed our love for him, and told him what he meant to us. I cried on and off all day as I remembered the day he was born, and his growing up years, and the future that he would not have. It was one of the saddest days of our lives. We got through it by the grace of God.

Our life was so hard. Jack and I knew one day our life would go back to "normal" but the cost, the trade-off was our son's death. It was too high a price to pay. Chris too paid a price to stay alive. He fought every day to maintain the life that he had, but the price was continuous and ever increasing physical pain and great emotional pain. Chris's pain would only end with death. But death was frightening, the unknown, the end of at least his physical relationships and involvement with everyone and everything that he loved, the end of everything as he knew it. He had to go alone, beyond death to face what? More pain? Judgment? Nothingness? Eternity? Heaven? Had he earned heaven? Forgiveness? God's love?

Chris fought to stay alive, supported by us, his family and by the wonderful team of nurses, physicians, lab technicians, and Steri-Pharm. He fought to stay alive because he was afraid to die. I sensed he needed to work out the answers to those questions before he would be ready.

Every night after he had turned on his side and was ready to go to sleep, Jack would go upstairs to bed and the nurse would return to the living room. As Chris requested, I would turn off the lights in the family room so that the only light coming in the room was a soft, low light from the kitchen. I would bring my chair close to Chris's bed so that we could talk without being overheard. Quietly we'd pray together and share our impressions of the day, our hopes, and our fears. Often Chris would raise these questions asking me what I thought.

One night after praying together he voiced his fears. He was afraid to die because he would not know anyone. The only thing I could think of to say was that he would know Jesus. Then I assured him that our love would never end; it would go with him into the next life. Until that moment I had not known or understood that. But at that moment I knew in my heart that it was true. I said, "I want you to know that I'll know where you are."

I was speaking from my heart and my soul and from my desperate desire to remain close to my son. As far as I know it was not based on any theological knowledge that I had acquired. I simply knew it was true.

Another night he voiced another fear. He said that he had not accomplished what he wanted to during his lifetime; therefore, he had not succeeded. He said, "I've spent all of my life learning and going to school and preparing for the future." He said, regretfully, "I haven't even been able to graduate from college and succeed at a career. I haven't had time to get married and have children." He felt that he had done nothing to merit eternal life.

These ideas added to his fear of dying. I replied that I thought he had accomplished so much. I told him that he had always had a desire to learn and a thirst for knowledge. I shared with him what I had been observing during the past year – that I had seen him grow spiritually and emotionally during the time he had been confined to his bed.

"You can't walk, and your body is getting sicker and deteriorating while your soul has become more beautiful, more loving. I see you in pain and you accept it and deal with it. You continue to make decisions about your life, even very hard ones and you don't complain about it. Each day you choose how to interact with Dad, the nurses and me. In spite of your problems you continue to express your concerns and fears for each of us and you give us your suggestions and input and most of all your love. You've had the courage to deal with your cancer. Your courage inspires us to be courageous too. I've seen you let go of so much that you love. Not only have you had to resign yourself to giving up your dreams for your future; but you have surmounted your own grief over your many losses and have had the courage to give your treasured possessions to the brother and sisters that you love so much. When your friends call, in spite of your realization that you no longer can share in their worlds, you still try to listen to them and advise them. Yet you don't put your sorrows on their shoulders."

I reminded him that at the University Hospital in October he had said, "Love is the only thing that matters."

I explained that some people live a lifetime and never learn that. I told him, "These are the accomplishments that the Lord sees. In the world of spirit you've climbed mountains."

Chris listened quietly without much comment, but I knew that he would reflect upon what I had said.

In the evenings when Chris would turn to me for answers to these questions, I'd silently beg for wisdom. I'd never counseled a dying person before and this was my son! I wanted him to have the best spiritual guide possible. I was not that person. I was inadequate for this privilege and responsibility. During our prayers and at Mass in the mornings, I'd implore Jesus for guidance so that I would know how to respond to Chris. I was his mother and friend; now I sensed he wanted me to be his spiritual advisor.

I had hoped that Chris would turn to Father Bertino, but although Father visited and offered his prayers and blessing, and our pastor, Father Dettmer brought him the Holy Eucharist each Monday morning, Chris did not encourage either of these priests to give him spiritual guidance. Chris seemed to be turning to me. Consequently, I needed and wanted to prepare Chris to die, to answer his questions, to give him courage and support. I wanted to walk with him as far as I could, and to help him to accept death and the end of his life, as he and I knew it. I needed to help him and me to know more about life after death. I wanted and needed to take away the fear, not only for him but also for me.

During those months, I read many books several of which dealt with terminal illness and death including Kubler-Ross's books. The one that helped me the most is, *Life after Life* by Raymond Moody, M.D. It was there exactly when I needed it. There are no accidents. When the pupil is ready, the teacher will come. The teacher for Chris and me was the shared experiences of countless people who had had near-death experiences. Dr. Moody interviewed them and found all of them had similar experiences. Most of them felt as though they had been pulled through a tunnel. As they came close to the end of the tunnel, they were drawn toward an intensely bright light, a being of light. But as bright as the light was, it didn't hurt their eyes. Those who were Christian thought the being of light was Jesus. But believers in life after death or not, all of them experienced the same feeling and sense of light. It was a personal being with a definite personality and a sense of humor. Upon reaching and feeling surrounded by the light, they felt intense love and warmth.

While this was happening, they also saw a review of their life, during which they even experienced the same emotions they had when the events originally occurred. The being of light pointed out the times when they had failed to show love. The review was not experienced as judgment; it was meant to help them to reflect on their lives and to teach rather than to condemn. They felt totally loved and accepted. They were asked similar questions in a thought-transference way in which there was no possibility of misunderstanding. They were asked if they were prepared to die. "What have you done with your life to show me?"

As they witnessed the review, the being of light seemed to express the importance of two things in life: learning to love and acquiring knowledge. They were given the impression that there would always be a quest for knowledge; it is a continuous process that goes on after death.

As this was occurring, the ND (near death) person was also aware of what was happening in the place in which he had "died." Those who had suffered cardiac arrest could describe in minute detail everything that was said and done to them. Those in car accidents and unconscious could read the thoughts of people that were a distance away. They tried to reassure family, friends, and medical personnel that they were fine. The only ones who wanted to come back were those who had a sense that they had to return to finish their work, such as mothers with young children. All of them lost their fear of dying.

This book, more than any other, strengthened my belief that at the moment of death Chris would go from our arms into the arms of Jesus. The message was an incredible revelation and affirmation of my belief in eternal life and confirmed my mother's own near-death experience at age eight. It helped me to understand what Chris would experience when his soul left his body. I drew great comfort from these ND experiences, because now I knew Jesus, the being of light, would meet him and immediately he would experience love, warmth, and acceptance.

Now I could respond to Chris's fear that he did not merit eternity in heaven or that he would go into nothingness or face a terrible judgment. I could tell him that the two questions that the being of light asked everyone were: have you learned to love others, and have you acquired knowledge. Without question these were two things that Chris had accomplished. Chris who "always wanted to make things better" was not demonstrative in the way he showed love. He did it with his actions, in his own way. Moreover, in the past year I had witnessed many examples of Chris's ability to love. I was to experience many more. He had spent his twenty-three years learning because he had a passion for it. Had he lived longer, I think he might have become a modern day renaissance man. As painful as it was going to be to go on living without Chris's physical presence, I knew that he would know joy and happiness when he died and met the being of light. That was what I wanted for him. At that moment I felt God's love for all of us, and my own love for God, the Comforter, grew and brought me comfort.

In October, when Chris came home from the hospital as a paraplegic with no hope of recovering, I made a "deal" with God. I told Him I understood that I was being called to help my son through his final stage of life with all the pain that it would entail. I would endure Chris's suffering and my own pain and do everything that I could to help Christopher. I would be there emotionally, physically, and spiritually. But at the moment of his death, "I want You to come and bring him home with You. I want Chris to go from our arms into Yours." Now God answered my prayers in a very concrete way, through the near-death experiences of people who could come back to share their experience with the living. Through them, He was telling us not to fear; He would be there to take Chris home.

I read the book in November and one night after our prayers,

I told Chris that I had read a book called, *Life After Life.* I was eager to share all that I had learned with Chris so that he would not be afraid to die and he would know what to expect. He responded with, "It isn't time yet."

GROWING IN LOVE – LETTING GO IN LOVE

The winter of 1987 was one of the mildest and sunniest that I can remember. The warm days tantalized Chris. He would look out of the window and pine to be out-doors. He'd complain, "Oh! If only I could smell the fresh air." I'd open the window furthest away from his bed in the hope he could smell the fresh air across the room. Because of his pre-carious health, I was afraid he might catch a cold. He still ran a fever most of the time which made him uncomfortably hot, soaking through his shirts and pillowcases several times a day. The hospital had generously supplied us with scrub shirts which I cut down the back and hemmed enabling Chris to remove them without discomfort. He had full mobility of his arms, hands, head and shoulders; but he had no feeling below his upper chest and consequently he could not move.

In January, Chris's condition seemed to stabilize. Days passed without any new infections or increase in pain. He seemed to be more cheerful, too. In fact, he even thought he would like to work with his computer. His first computer, an Osbourne, was small enough to sit on his tray table. He wanted to write a pro-gram for Jack so that he could keep track of his tax deductions during the year, thereby making it easier for him at income tax time. Each afternoon after lunch, I would set up the computer on his tray table so that he could work at it. The nurses and I were delighted to see him lose himself in work that he loved. However, one afternoon a week later, a new very sharp pain began in his upper back necessitating an increase in morphine. He was unable to use the computer that day and he never again felt well enough to finish the program, because he seemed to decline more rapidly after that period of stability.

One day in March, Chris told me he wanted to leave everything he had to John, Maryann and Michele. He had given it careful thought, and he knew how he wanted to divide up his material possessions. They consisted of his two-year-old Honda, his pride and joy, some stock that had increased in value, an IRA he funded while working at the steel mills for a summer, a MacIntosh computer and printer, and a set of Lionel and HO trains that belonged to him and John. Chris wanted to give his car and computer to John; but John had recently bought a used Saab and didn't need a car; however he needed a computer and printer and he wanted the train set as well. Since John didn't need the CRX, Chris decided to sell it along with the stock. He also wanted to withdraw the money in the IRA and close the account. Within two days Jack sold the car to a colleague who bought it for his college age son, we arranged to sell the stock, and I took a letter of direction from Chris to the bank and withdrew his IRA money. At his direction I opened an account in my name and put all of Chris's money into it. When Michele and Maryann came home that weekend, he told each of them that the money in the account and any accrued interest was his gift to them. He wanted them to keep it in the account until they were ready to buy their first home. In this way, he felt he would be contributing to and participating in their future.

This son of ours continued to overwhelm us with love and generosity. He had made an incredibly difficult and loving decision. He put himself through the difficult task of making out his last will and executing it. The maturity of our 23-year-old son was at once touching and painful. What inner strength and courage! What a beautiful, loving spirit! I sensed he was working out his eternity in that bed because physically and emotionally it was Calvary and the crucifixion. I watched him quietly think things through and then make the necessary decisions. They were conscious acts. Each time he did this he had to let go of something: a physical ability, a material possession, or an aspect of his health.

Caring for Chris and being with him each day was our gift and privilege. But it didn't come easily. Every time I looked at Chris in that hospital bed I died a little. It was torture to see him day after day confined to a bed, his lifeless legs straight out in front of him, his body surrounded by pillows to protect his fragile spine, his big brown eyes sad and hopeless. His hair, once so thick was shedding and could only be washed with a dry hair shampoo. His once handsome face, now thin and sallow, had a tumor the size of a walnut protruding from his left temple. He was limited to just a few movements. He could move his head from side to side and raise is arms, but turning on his side was impossible without two people and a draw sheet. He could only sit up part way because edema caused his abdomen and lower body to swell to the extent that he could not bend at the waist. But in spite of all of his hardships he was still in charge.

For months Jack and I had lived with constant high level emotional distress -Jack even more so because he also had the responsibility of a practice. But we had learned to survive at that level. I was not aware of myself physically any more. My body simply moved mechanically rarely complaining about the long hours and interrupted sleep. The only pain I was aware of was the pain of seeing my son dying, and even that paled next to Chris's suffering and loss.

Our friends felt sorry for us because we didn't have any time to spend away from Chris. They couldn't know that we were where we wanted to be – consciously living each moment. We were painfully but fully alive being with Christopher. It was our privilege to be able to share ideas, listen to him speak, observe and admire his courage. We were imprinting his face, voice and ideas into our brains for the rest of our lives. We were creating memories, giving and receiving love, praying together, drawing strength and courage from each other and sharing our pain. We shared our sadness, our fears, and our regrets. We were grieving together, apologizing for hurting each other, bonding together. It was our finest moment as human beings.

In early April, about three weeks before he died, when he felt he was ready, he asked me to read *Life After Life* to him. I read it to him in two days because he was in a hurry to have me finish the book. His internal clock was telling him that it was time. When I read the passage in which the being of light asked each of the persons who had "died" if they had learned to love other people and if they had acquired knowledge, Chris asked me to read the passage several times to make sure he understood it correctly. When I finished, he said, "Then I've won, Mom."

I said, "Yes, Chris, you've won." He seemed to lose his fear of dying then, or so it seemed to me because he deteriorated very rapidly after that.

At 6:30 a.m. on the morning of May 4th, I helped to turn Chris, then dressed and went to Mass. I came home and as usual I quietly entered the family room and asked Christopher if he was ready to sit up. He said that he wasn't ready yet. For the last three weeks he had been sleeping longer and longer because he was so weak and sick.

I went upstairs, made my daily call to my parents, and wrote in my journal. Each day as I looked at my son and cared for him, I knew our time together was drawing to an end. I wanted his suffering to be over, but at the same time, the pain of separation would only be beginning for us, and I didn't want to face life without Chris. I fervently wished, as I had for weeks, that I could go with Chris – to die with him so that I would not be separated from him.

At Mass that morning as I went up to communion, I asked Jesus again to take Christopher. But this time I said, "I want you to take him," rather than "Chris is ready to die; he wants you to take him." He had suffered so much, I would not hold on to him and have him suffer any longer than he already had.

Journal Entry • Monday, May 4, 1987

I went to Mass in the chapel at Notre Dame church this morning. As I looked at the image of Christ on the cross, I noticed how his chest was expanded and stretched abnormally. I immediately thought of Chris's chest and realized the similarity between the two. But the similarity goes much further, to the core, to suffering itself. Earlier in the Mass a scripture passage stated, "Christ is present in every suffering." That comforts me so. I want Christ present every moment to Chris and to all of us. I look at Jesus on the cross and wonder how he can hold all of mankind's suffering. One has to be God to endure it – and God to understand the value of it. Only God could endure such absolute suffering – the anguish of humanity and the problem of pain and suffering. Is pain necessary to the growth of our spirit?

As I continued to look at the image of Christ on the cross, I became aware of the dignity with which he suffered. Again, I see a similarity. Chris is suffering and dying with dignity – quietly, gently, in spite of deep pain. I thought of Mother Theresa – how she helps the poor to die with dignity. Dying with dignity is not the least we can give a dying person; it is the most we can give. I wish this for every dying person, those with cancer, AIDS, those in wars. If only we could offer this to each person during life's transition to another life!

I look at Chris, so altered physically, the look of emaciation, starvation. He has had no solid food for one month now, and only a piece of toast and an egg a day for two or three weeks before that. For the last week, he hasn't even had any milk shakes. But he drinks about a quart of milk a day. He has the look of someone who has been in a concentration camp. But when he and I talk, when he looks at me with those big, open, sad, tired eyes, I see my son, Christopher. There is no pretense between us, only honesty – spoken and unspoken. I know his pain and he knows mine. We are so close! Such a great privilege – intense bonding – our finest moment. To get there I had to be willing to endure the pain of being present to Chris, dealing with my feelings and allowing them to surface. I've been there emotionally almost all of the

time, whenever Chris wanted to talk. I haven't repressed my feel-
ings to him or to myself. I know this is a gift, but the gift could
not be experienced without experiencing the pain. As I see and
care for Chris, I continue to realize that it is a privilege to minister
to someone, especially to my son who is dying and who is working
toward sainthood.

Pain has to be meritorious; otherwise what would be the purpose
for it? I feel he is participating in the redemption of souls. Our
Christopher, the Christ bearer. Was this ordained from eternity?
Wasn't the choice of the name Christopher appropriate? We had
no plans to name him Christopher, but the name came to me from
out of the blue shortly before he was born, and very suddenly, Jack
and I felt it was the perfect name for him. I see that it was.

Chris didn't want to be lifted into a sitting position until
10:00 a.m. that morning. I opened the drapes and took away
the bedside intercom that he used to call me in the middle of
the night when he was ready to turn to a different position.
With the nurse's help, we turned Chris and raised the bed so he
could sit up partially upright. Marsha placed his pills and water
in front of him. Slowly, in the next half-hour, he managed to
get them down. A little later, he was able to drink some milk.
All his movements had become slow and deliberate, as though
he had to concentrate on every movement. As I watched him,
I remembered how Jack and I would watch with pride as Chris
used his highly developed motor skills to build things so pre-
cisely. Now, still using the concentration he had developed, he
was still able to care for himself and to change the morphine
cartridge on his Hickman pump, but the dexterity was no
longer there and he had to concentrate very hard to make his
hands respond. His thin fingers and arms bore no resemblance
to my son's.

Sitting next to him watching him grow sicker and sicker
was tearing me apart. Chris knew it. He knew that his time
with us was coming to an end. But he didn't allow himself to

cry. In the months that we had been at home I had not seen him cry. Because he was paralyzed up to his chest, he was unable to take deep breaths. He told me soon after we came home from the hospital that crying made him feel that he was suffocating. Even the small comfort and release that tears could bring were not possible for him.

That morning I asked if I could wash his face. He nodded his head. Words were difficult for him now. I gently wiped his face and hands with water. I cried, kissed his hand and told him that I loved him, as I had so often before. He slowly raised his head, looked at me with eyes barely open and focused and mouthed the words back to me, "I love you." I returned to my chair next to his bed and we simply sat together as we had for all those months.

For the last several days, Chris had been too weak and too sick to carry on a conversation. He wasn't able to watch television, although he usually wanted the set on and the volume low. He was still in charge. He decided when he wanted to turn and drink something nourishing.

He always wanted me to sit next to him even though few words were exchanged now. I was grateful that this brought him some comfort. He still managed to open his eyes and give Jack a little smile when he came home at lunch time to spend an hour with him. But we were no longer able to carry on long conversations with him or share our thoughts. He was letting go and moving away from us. As much as we wanted to hang on to him; we were being forced to let him go. It was horrifying to come face to face with the inevitable - we were losing him, and we would be left behind. We were not going to be able to make the rest of the journey with him. Our son had to make the rest of the journey alone. We, his family whom he loved and who loved him, could not go on with him.

Three weeks before, he had said, "I don't want to do this any more." The week before he told me, "I want to get out of here," and then, "How much longer do I have to do this?"

Tearfully, I had responded, "It will be soon, Chris, very soon."

When he said, "thank you" in response, it nearly broke my heart.

Tears fell in a continuous stream as I sat next to him the morning of May 4th and watched him as he lay dying. I looked at his beautiful face, imprinting it in my memory for the lonely years ahead. Once in a while, Chris would open his eyes and slowly turn his head to look at me. At one point, he motioned to me to hold his hand. I knew it was to comfort me rather than the reverse. During the last weeks, I had dreaded thinking about life without Chris. Now, in pain and anguish, I said, "How will I live without you?" Chris had no response. He only looked at me sadly and silently.

A few weeks before, I had asked Chris to come for me when it was my turn to die. He had responded, "If they'll let me."

Chris had always kept a careful eye on the morphine level left in his pump so that he could plan to replace it when he was in a sitting position. May 4th was no exception. Although he could barely speak, he asked me to have Marsha get a full morphine cartridge from the refrigerator. Carefully and slowly he replaced the cartridge and Marsha took away the empty one.

The day before, I had asked Chris again if Nana Luce could come to see him on Monday. He had been reluctant to have her come often, because when she was under stress, as she was when she visited Chris, she had a tendency to speak endlessly about inconsequential things in an effort to distract herself from the truth about her grandson's health. Her lack of sensitivity was difficult for Chris to handle; consequently he didn't want her to visit. But yesterday he had consented, and Jack planned to bring her over after the morning surgical procedures. However, that Monday morning Jack remained in the hospital for a delivery, necessitating a postponement of Nana's visit until the next morning.

John, Michele, Maryann and her family had come to see Chris during the past weekend. They knew by his altered condition that he would not be with us very much longer. It was a terrible weekend knowing that this was probably our last time together as a family. Each of them said tearful good-byes to him realizing that they might not see him again. As difficult as it was to leave him and to drive away, each of them had jobs and duties to which they had to return.

On Monday mornings Father Dettmer always came to give Chris the Holy Eucharist and to pray briefly with him. But Father was on vacation this week and he would not be coming.

At around 1:00 p.m. Chris said he was ready to go down on his side. I called Marsha, and together we carefully lowered the bed, lifted Chris to one side, and then used the draw-sheet to turn him on his side replacing the pillows he needed to support his back and chest. I stayed with him as he slept and watched my beautiful son. At 3:00 p.m. Vicki came and Marsha left.

When Jack came home, we lifted Chris to a sitting position, and sat with him. Around 4:30 p.m. Chris replaced the morphine cartridge again. He was using large doses now. We were too grief stricken to do anything but look at Chris and at each other and cry. For more than a year, the three of us had been almost inseparable. We had shared so much and spent so much time together in the family room. It had been a place of great physical and emotional pain, but it had also been a place where love and joy had been exchanged. Soon, our vigil would be over, and we would have a "normal" life: but to experience that, we had to give up our beloved son and brother - an unspeakable abomination.

A little past 7:00 p.m. I became aware that he was having difficulty breathing. Jack and Vicki came in and took his vital signs. His lungs were filled with fluid; he had pneumonia. The time I had dreaded, worried, and cried about, our time of separation, Chris's last agony, was upon us. With Vicki's help we brought the portable oxygen tank into the room and using a nasal cannula placed him on oxygen.

Months before Jack had insisted that we talk about this

moment. Painfully, we had come to the realization that we did not want Chris rushed to the hospital for heroic measures that would only prolong his suffering. We wanted him to be with us as long as possible, but not if it meant his suffering would escalate. In the last seven and a half months, Chris, Jack, the medical personnel, and I had fought hard to overcome every infection Chris had had. But we believed that when the time came, we would know it, and as hard as it would be, we would not panic and try heroic measures. We wanted Chris to die as naturally and gently as possible in the home he had loved and lived in since he was four.

We knew that Chris was ready. But I wasn't. Even though at Mass that morning I had told Jesus that I wanted him to take Chris; I would never be ready to let him go. He had become my entire life. And now I had only a few hours left to be with him and to take care of him. I could not fall apart. Not now while Chris still needed me. I would accompany him until I could go no further and until he met the being of light. Months ago I had made a commitment to God that I would accept His will for Chris, but I wanted Chris to go from our arms directly into His. Now it was time. That was my focus that night, and what made it possible for me to get through that agonizing heart breaking ordeal. Soon Chris would be in the arms of God where he would be free and gloriously happy. His agony was almost over. At that moment nothing else mattered, not my fear, not my loss, only Chris mattered.

I was very frightened. I didn't know what would be happening in the next few hours, and how much Chris's suffering would increase. At that moment I needed to pray. I took out my rosary and knelt down beside Chris's bed. But I prayed by rote because my mind and heart were on Chris. I looked at him in disbelief that he was actually dying. My mind was having difficulty understanding that. I looked around at this room that, since the age of four, had been an important part of Chris's life as a playroom, family room, a hospital room, and now as

the room in which he would die. I saw the little four year playing on the floor, and the fourteen year old stretched out in front
of the TV with our dog at his side. I saw him playing games
with Maryann, Michele, and John. I saw him sitting with Ann
on the sofa smiling and happy. The walls echoed with sounds
of laughter, arguments, discussions, tears, joys, and sorrows –
truly a room where a family lived – and died. Chris's death
would be physical; ours would be emotional as we endured the
pain of having Chris wrenched from our arms by this terrible
disease that was claiming his young and precious life.

My strong Jack, despite his own grief, took care of the necessary things. He called Dr. Paul who agreed that it looked like
the end was near and that all we could do was to keep him
comfortable. This meant that I might need to increase the
morphine and later in the evening, at 10:30 I would have to
change the morphine pump by myself. Chris and I had
changed the pump at about 4:00 p.m., but I had never actually
done all of it myself without Chris's supervision. For all of
these months, I had known that I would need to know how to
change the morphine cartridge when he could no longer do it.
I watched him frequently so that I could do it when the time
came. But now I was afraid that in my present state of mind,
I might make a mistake programming it and Chris would be
without the needed morphine during this most crucial time.

I called Willie, our pharmacist, and told him the situation,
and asked him if he would stay on the phone with me when it
was time to change the pump. This compassionate man, who
had never failed to help us during the past months, assured me
he would talk me through it when I needed to change the pump.

Thank God for Jack's strength. He was the one who called
John, Maryann, and Michele and told them that their brother
was dying. He told them to pack some things and he would call
them later if Chris's condition worsened rapidly. We asked
John to drive to the western suburb where Michele lived so that
neither of them would have to be alone during the difficult

drive home. Maryann and Dave would not leave until morning because of the two babies.

At 8:00 p.m. Chris grabbed the pump and started reprogramming it. I tried to tell him the pump was okay, but he seemed to panic. He didn't understand me. Finally, I said, "Please Chris, I'll take care of it; the pump is okay right now." And he understood me. He said okay in a high squeaky voice because he had so little oxygen left in his lungs. I was afraid he would mess it up and I would be unable to rectify it. Thinking that Chris had wanted to increase the dosage, Jack suggested that I increase the amount of his hourly dosage to 92 mg. per hour. We didn't want to increase it too much because we didn't want to overdose him, yet we wanted him to be comfortable. Comfortable! What an inappropriate word. I remembered that when he came home from the hospital in October his hourly dosage was 4 mg. per hour. During those months, Chris had gradually had to increase the dosage to block out the ever-increasing pain.

Jack and I cried quietly as we knelt at his bed and prayed for him. Every half-hour, Vicki came in and gently took his pulse. His pressure was dropping from 120, to 110, to 100. Chris had his eyes closed, but he could hear us. Forgetting that Father Dettmer was out of the city, I asked him if he wanted me to call for Father. Chris said no. He had had the Last Rites a week ago when Father had come.

We tried to keep him comfortable. Chris was still on his back, partially upright. I kept thinking that it was time for Chris to turn on his side because he had been on his back too long and we had to be concerned about pressure points. I had to tell myself that Chris was dying, sadly pressure points no longer mattered. I held on to his hand; trying to feel and to hold on to the life that was still there but slowly ebbing away. I looked down at his fingers that had been so adept and agile and now lay motionless in my palm, and I grieved for all the projects that he would not have the joy of doing. Those hands

that would never again hold a hammer, work on a project, photograph a sunset, drive a car, hold a girl's hand, lift a child of his
into his arms. The end of his dreams, the end of his future.
The end of hope. All the months of fear, anxiety, prayerful
hope, all the months of witnessing Christopher's courage in the
face of such terrible emotional and physical pain were coming
to an end. For his sake I wanted it to be over. But it was
unbearable to know that Chris would no longer be here with
Maryann, Michele, John, Jack and I.

Jack on one side of his bed and I on the other stayed with
him, spoke gently, assured him that we were there with him.
I told him how much I loved him. I thanked him for being our
son, for the joy he had given us. I told him Jesus loved him and
that He was waiting for him with open arms.

At about midnight, Chris had a seizure. We tried to take hold
of his hands, but with surprising force, he pushed our hands
away. His body stiffened, then his arms became limp and his
fingers contorted. After the seizure, Chris did not seem to hear
us, but his eyes were wide open now. I stood in such a way
that, if he could see he would be able to look at me. I didn't
want him to think he was alone. I held his hand, kissing it,
talking to him, assuring him. Jack, on his other side spoke softly to him, thanking him for being our son and for all that he
had done for us through the years, for always wanting to make
things better. I told him I would miss him. Our love for one
another would never end; it would increase. Our love would
go with him into eternity. I told him again that I would know
where he was. I assured him that he would be very happy and
that he would continue to learn. We asked him to pray for us.
Jack and I asked him again to please come for us when it was
our time to die. We didn't know how much he understood, but
if he was aware, we wanted him to know we were with him
until he met the being of light, Jesus.

Jack called the children back and asked them to come.
At 2:30 a.m. Jack called my friend, Terese who had offered to

come to be with us during Chris's last hours. She and Vicki
prayed together in the living room and from time to time came
into the family room to offer their support and assistance. Vicki
thought that he was no longer feeling pain; but not knowing if
he was she reminded me every half hour to give him a bolus
dose of morphine. Jack finally sat down and dozed briefly,
because he was exhausted having been up most of the previous
night delivering a baby, and had cared for his patients all day.
Jack had brought several thousand children into the world; but
sadly, he was helpless to prevent his son from leaving it.

I stood at Chris's left side. I looked at his wonderful eyes as
he stared back at me. I had such a short time left to look at
him, to hold his hand, to talk to him, and to take care of him.
I treasured every moment. As heart breaking as it was to see
him this way, I couldn't move my eyes away from his face.
Around 4:00 a.m. he raised his hand and removed the oxygen
tubing from his nose. We thought he didn't know what he was
doing. Later, I realized he couldn't talk anymore but he was
telling us that the oxygen wasn't helping anymore. I am heart
broken that I didn't understand in spite of his great effort to
communicate. I talked to him and replaced it. He must have
given up trying to explain. What an effort it must have been to
raise his hand and remove the cannula.

Now I realized that he could hear me. I stood the rest of the
night with my right arm behind his pillow, cradling his head,
and holding his left hand. His eyes were focused on my face as
I talked quietly to him through the night. I don't know if he
really saw me; I want to think that he did. I kept looking into
his face wanting to imprint his eyes in my memory.

Weeks before I told Terese that I was afraid of our last
moment together. I didn't think I could go through it. She
assured me that I could — that I would be so completely
involved with Chris that I wouldn't fall apart. She was right.
I wanted to ease Chris's suffering; I focused on him. I told him
that he could let go, "Jesus loves you. We all love you very

much. Thank you for being our love, for being my friend. I'll know where you are. Jesus is waiting for you with open arms. Don't be afraid." He continued to stare into my eyes.

In spite of the last year and a half, I could not believe I was holding my dying son. This was actually happening to my son, my friend. His breathing had been labored and now an awful death rattle began. It was the worst torture to watch helplessly as our son's life ebbed away. I wanted to take his place. I desperately wanted his agony, his pain and suffering to end. I knew that the end was near. Wave after wave of grief washed over me. I kept repeating "Oh Chris!" But I could not allow my own agony to overwhelm me. I remained focused on Chris because I wanted to be with him, to be his mother, his strength until Jesus came and freed him from all of this life's pain and suffering.

If we were not already bonded together as mother and son, his illness, our verbal and silent sharing, our mutual suffering, have bound us together for eternity. I told him during those quiet talks at night that the love we all had for each other would never end. It would go on for eternity. He would bring our love with him into the next life, and he would bring all that he had learned. All of his knowledge would go with him, and he would continue to learn and to love. He agreed with me that our love for each other would never end. Now at his deathbed, I was letting go of him physically, but I knew that spiritually we would always be together because nothing separates us in the world of the spirit. During those hours, I began to understand that a part of me, my spirit, would always be connected to Chris.

Sometime during the early hours, Jack called our parents and told them to come. We hoped the children would make it before he died. As day approached, his breathing became slower and slower. We spoke softly and held him close to us with sorrow that was beyond tears. His last breath was near. When he died; he would be drawn toward Jesus, the being of light, but he still would be able to see us and know what was happening on the physical plane.

He drew his last breath at 6:50 a.m. on May 5th. In numerology five is the symbol for love. Chris died on the fifth day of the fifth month. It was a bright, beautiful, sunny day in May. The flowers in the garden; phlox, azaleas, tulips, iris were all in bloom. And Chris was with Jesus. He had come through his agony, his cross. He was loved and with Jesus. Terese and Vicki left us alone, and Jack and I held him together for the last hour or more and we were holding him when Jesus came for him. It was appropriate that the four of us were together at his last moment on earth. We had been together at his creation.

It was a peaceful moment, a holy moment. I continued to hold Chris's hand, and stroked his hair. I kissed his hands. I hugged him. I simply sat with him. I looked around the room, in the doorways, and up toward the ceiling. I knew Chris was in the room looking at all of us, trying to tell us he was okay. He knew that I knew he was okay.

When Chris breathed his last breath, an irreparable stillness came over him. His body was still; his soul had left. The physical part of him was there, but his immortal soul had left his body forever and was now FREE. FREE of physical infirmities, of cancer, of paraplegia, of incontinence. Chris was out of his hospital bed. FREE! Free to be more loving, more Christopher than he had ever been. Not less – MORE!

I continued to sit with Chris as I had done for all the months that he had been paralyzed. I had no where else to go. I belonged at his side. I looked around the room hoping I would see Chris smiling and looking down at me. But I didn't. I kept looking at his face and hands that were now so still but at peace. It was over for Chris.

Some time later, Jack and I removed Chris's anti-embolism stockings and disconnected the pump that for more than seven months had provided a great measure of comfort. I told Vicki that I wanted a basin of water so I could wash his face and hands and arms. My last act as his mother. I would not let his face be covered. I continued to sit next to him as I held his hand

and stroked his hair. I was numb but at peace because Chris was no longer in pain. At that moment that was all that mattered. He had finished his ordeal and he was now with Jesus.

Jack's mother and sister, Betty arrived too late to see him alive. Mom stood looking at Chris quietly crying - her heart filled with the things she would have wanted to say to Chris. Friends came in soon after. They all went quietly into the living room. I remained with Chris – a quiet place. Where else would I have wanted to be? Too soon we would be separated.

Bill, our friend and funeral director, came at 8:30 a.m. With tears in his eyes, he came over to where I was sitting holding Chris's hand. He put Chris on the cart and started to cover Chris's face. But I made him stop. When my children leave the house for school or to travel, I always make the sign of the cross on their foreheads and say, "God go with you." My Italian grandmother always said, "God accompanies you," whenever we left the house. Chris was leaving the house on his last journey. I needed to bless him on his way. I made the sign of the cross on his forehead, kissed him, and whispered in Italian, "A Dio, filio mio." And then I had to let him go.

I stepped outside and watched as Bill drove slowly down Garden Trail and disappeared down the winding street. When my children left home to return to college, I always watched until their cars could no longer be seen. I was heartbroken knowing that this was the last time that I would watch Chris slowly disappear down Garden Trail.

I felt heaviness in my heart and in my entire body. But as I stood outside I noticed that it was a beautiful day for Chris's rebirth day. He was fine now because his suffering was over; he was happy and safe, and he was with Jesus. It was my consolation. I knew where he was and I knew that he and I would remain bonded.

Dazed and numb I stood in our small courtyard and gradually became aware of all the life forms around me. The ivy at my feet seemed filled with energy, teaming with life. I looked up at the honey locust tree and heard a bird sing and caught a glimpse of a butterfly. I became aware of all the tiny sparks of life, the insects in the ivy and the soil each held a spark of precious life. At that moment I understood how precious life is to the body, even to the tiny spark of life in an insect and a plant. That spark comes from the Creator; it is the breath of God. I had witnessed the difference between life and death. At that moment my respect for all life increased tremendously.

TRANSITION – LIVING WITH GRIEF –
LEARNING THROUGH GRIEF

Prayer Service given by Terese Fabbri
May 7th 1987
For Christopher Luce, his family, relatives, and friends:

"Each of us sees reality through our own eyes. I would like to share with you this evening the reality of Christopher Luce and his life this past year as I have seen it through my eyes. We've often been told as Christians that Jesus, the Son of God, came to earth and became a man so that we who saw him would also be seeing the Father. I would like to think that Chris Luce, a loving spirit, came to earth so that we who saw him would be seeing Love, would be seeing Jesus and the Father who are Love. I say this because in the past year of sharing – especially with his mother, Therese, that is what I saw most of all – Love. It seems to me that Chris drew love out of each person who spent any amount of time with him. Many things took place in his room – the family room – but for me what was most visible was the exchange of Love. Could it be that he was there to teach us about love and how to love? How well his family learned as they lovingly responded to him and his every need – day after day – never faltering, never quitting – always loving.

I was privileged to be with Therese and Chris and Jack those last few hours when Christopher made his transition from this earthly life to his new heavenly life. It was during this time that I learned about accomplishments. You know, accomplishing something with our lives is an issue for most of us. It is something we all want to do – and Chris was no different. He would ask Therese at times about his accomplishing something. It seemed to him that all he did was go to school – he was in training a great deal of the time – almost his whole life! What had he accomplished? This is what I learned about Chris's accomplishments as I watched and waited with him and his parents.

I listened to Vicki, one of his nurses, who while holding Chris's hand expressed her thanks for being able to take care of Chris and be with him at that very special time. I heard her tell all the lessons she learned from Chris – how she learned to be patient as she watched him grow in patience – how she learned about letting go as she watched him let go of one thing after another – how she learned to be gentle in her touch and to watch for and be sensitive to Chris and his feelings. And, finally, I heard her say how different she is now at home with her husband and her child – how she has slowed down, how she is more patient, how she is so much more aware of them and their needs and their feelings, how much better she knows them for who they are.

Perhaps it is because I am a teacher and have been one for so long that this touched me so deeply. What I came to see so clearly was that Chris accomplished every teacher's dream: to so touch their students' lives that they would change – that they would grow – that they would be better because their paths had crossed in the classroom. For me, Chris was a teacher of the highest caliber – he touched so many lives with his person that each one grew, each one changed, each one became better because their path crossed his at some point in time, and they would never be the same.

I want to thank Jack and Therese for bringing Chris into this world, and his brother, John – and his sisters Maryann and Michele, and his grandparents, who along with Therese and Jack loved and nurtured him, taught him and led him to be the teacher he is. May you, his family, continue his work and keep his Spirit of Love alive in you."

It was a tribute to Chris that several hundred people came to the wake to pay their last respects. What helped me to get through the wake was the knowledge and sense that Chris's spirit was there with me, not immobilized in the casket, but free and very present. It was my comfort as I spoke to so many people that day.

During the wake I told many people that expressed their sympathy, that Chris's ordeal was over and that "he is fine now." One of those with whom I spoke was a friend of Maryann's, a behavioral psychologist. Days later, Maryann told me that her friend had come up to her after speaking with me and said, "Your mother is off the wall."

I remembered that I had told her friend that, "Chris is fine now," and repeated this to Maryann.

Her response was, "Well, Mother, no wonder she said you were off the wall, she doesn't believe in God or in an after life."

Perhaps other people thought I was off the wall that day. It's been said that if someone doesn't believe, nothing will convince them and if they believe, no explanation is necessary.

His funeral Mass was a celebration of his life with five priests at the altar, and the choir singing the beautiful and moving hymns that John and I had selected: "On Eagles Wings" and "Here I Am Lord." Rather than sit woodenly in the pew, I took part in the beautiful prayers being said for Chris; because I wanted to actively participate in the celebration of Chris's going home to the Father.

Since his death, I had reflected on how I could continue to be of help to Chris now. I sensed that I could help by giving him back to the Creator who gave him to us twenty-three years before. I wanted to release him completely, with an open and loving heart, so that having completed his earthly life, he would be free to fully experience the joys of his new life and continue his journey in love and knowledge. As I participated in the prayers of the Mass, I kept this intention in mind as I prayed that nothing would hold Chris back from the joy and wonder of his new life.

Maryann, dressed in white because she was celebrating the life of her brother who had become a saint, went up to the lectern and read the First Reading in a trembling voice. Michele went to the lectern next and in a clear voice read the Responsorial Psalm. John went up to the lectern for the Second Reading. With faltering voice, many pauses, and tears he struggled to get through the reading. With incredible willpower he was able to finish. When he returned to the pew in which we were sitting he broke down completely and Michele, the one that Chris had worried about, put her arms around John and consoled him. The night after his death, she had dreamed of Chris, happy and smiling, wearing his blue oxford shirt, standing in a group of men talking with Albert Einstein. That dream convinced her that Chris wanted her to know that he was happy, safe, and in the arms of the Lord, and it gave her the strength she needed to endure her terrible loss.

When Maryann and Dave came home the day of Chris's death they brought the chalice and ciborium inscribed with Chris's name which they had quietly purchased the previous Christmas. Now at the Mass, the celebrant, Father Bertino, Chris's friend read the blessing for the chalice and ciborium and said, "What gift do you give to your brother at Christmas when you know he is dying? If you are Maryann and Dave, you give him a chalice and ciborium which after this Mass will be sent to a missionary priest in Chris's memory." It has been comforting to know that this gift for Chris will last as long as a missionary priest uses it, because he will pray for his benefactors and for their intentions whenever he uses the chalice and ciborium at Mass.

At the cemetery, as Father Bertino with tears in his eyes prayed, "Father, accept your servant Christopher..," I held out my hands in a symbol of giving him back to the Father. I did

not want to hold on to him, lest I keep him from fully participating in his new life and rebirth. When the prayers were over,
Chris's Phi Kappa Psi fraternity brothers, each holding a red
rose, gathered around his casket as Mark, the fraternity president led them in the moving Phi Kappa Psi burial service. We
were so grateful that these young men were present to honor
him as one of their own. I know that Chris was looking down
at them, so pleased to be honored by these brothers who meant
so much to him.

After the luncheon I spoke with all of the magnificent young
fraternity and sorority men and women and thanked them for
their presence. As I said good-by to them and they turned to
walk away I wanted to shout, "Wait for Chris, he's coming too."

It was so difficult to acknowledge the difference between
these young men and women and our son who lay dead. Their
faces held such promise for the future. They would graduate,
marry, have children, and continue their friendships. We would
never attend Chris's graduation. He would not escort me down
the isle at John's and Michele's weddings as he had at
Maryann's. We would not celebrate his wedding nor have the
joy of loving his wife and children. Chris's life on earth was
over. Only memories would sustain us now.

By the time the luncheon was over I felt a pull to return to
our family room. I simply wanted to go home and sit quietly in
the family room. I couldn't wait to get back. But it was not to
be, because at that moment my mother became ill and was
taken to the convenience clinic. John, Michele, and I brought
the two infants home and cared for them while we waited for
the rest of the family to return; consequently it wasn't possible
to sit quietly and reflect. Two hours later, when my mother was
hospitalized, I accompanied my eighty-six year old father to the
hospital, because having just buried his grandson, I was not
sure he could handle another crisis.

When my mother's problem was finally diagnosed as grief
and acute gastritis and she would recover, I came home with

Maryann and Dave. By that time it was 7:00 p.m. and little David and Nicole needed to be put to bed. I offered to give three month old Nicole her bottle while Maryann and Dave took care of David. The desire to return to the family room had never left me, and now I sat down on the sofa in the family room and began to give Nicole her bottle.

I was irritable and agitated, because I had not been able to spend the afternoon of our son's funeral sitting in the family room quietly grieving. I closed my eyes and tried to take some deep, relaxing breaths. What occurred in the next few seconds or minutes is difficult to relate because it still seems unbelievable to me. As I closed my eyes, it seemed as though a feeling injected itself into my thoughts, as though the thought or feeling was being done to me and I was feeling it. I had felt agitated and irritable, but as soon as I closed my eyes, a completely opposite feeling interrupted those feelings. The feeling or action if I can call it that seemed to originate from the right of where I was sitting. I believe that Chris was in the room and standing to my right. It was to be the first of many visits from Chris.

As I closed my eyes, my thoughts had turned to Chris, but that in itself was not unusual, because I always thought of him. However, this time as soon as I thought of him something incredible occurred. I immediately felt love between Chris and me so intensely that I became euphoric. A feeling of rapture and joy came over me. With these feelings came the awareness that there was no separation between us now. Thoughts and feelings could flow easily between us without misunderstanding, because there were no barriers any longer! The shocking words that came to me were "Oh! This is better now!" It came as an incredibly wonderful surprise!

Although I was sitting still, there was a feeling of movement as though I was being carried. I groped for a long time for a word to describe that feeling, and the one that best fits what I experienced is the word transported. There was also a sense of warmth and love. The room too seemed to be filled with love, with energy. As I experienced the sense of movement and euphoria, my next thought was "What's happening?" As that thought came to me the feeling of euphoria and joy slowly left me, and I sat in wonder no longer agitated or angry. I opened my eyes and looked at Nicole who was quietly drinking her bottle.

I was overwhelmed and marveled at what had just happened. God really loved us, beneficently allowing Christopher to return and reveal that our love for each other would continue, and that he would hear me when I thought of him. He was telling me that he would be able to communicate with me too because there is no separation, and that was an even greater gift.

Because I believe that Chris hears me, I often turn to him for insight. When I'm unsure how to respond to a problem or situation, I ask myself, "How would Chris want me to handle this?" The answer immediately becomes crystal clear. It is always to respond in the most loving way. The answers seem to be coming through my higher self rather than through my ego.

Our magnificent God was affirming that what I had told Chris during our quiet times together was true – that our love would never end. Now He was telling me how love works after a loved one has made the transition into the next life. Love flows between those we love, even those who have died and left their earthly bodies. Love is energy. And that energy continues to flow. Through thoughts and feelings that cannot be misunderstood we can now communicate on a higher level.

A few hours before I had given our son back to God, and the awesome God had generously and graciously given him back to me through this message. He knew how difficult it had been to take care of Chris, to endure his suffering and to lose him, and now He was gifting me by bringing Chris back to tell me that there was no separation between us. I understood then the reason why all afternoon I had had a strong drive to return to the family room.

When I awoke the next morning, my first semiconscious thought was that Chris had died. I would not be able to see him or to take care of him. There was a hole in my life that no one else could fill and I was overcome with emptiness and grief. Then I remembered the beautiful message that I had received the night before, and although I felt sorrow and emptiness, I was at peace and profoundly grateful.

At Mass that morning, I thanked Jesus, the Being of Light, for coming for Chris and for watching over us during Chris's long and painful illness. I thanked Chris for his visit of the night before, and thanked God for a better understanding of how deeply He loved us.

As I reflected on the experience, I began to understand that besides affirming our belief that Chris was now enjoying a new life in the spirit, the experience was given to help alleviate the pain of losing Chris's physical presence in our lives. I was being encouraged to elevate my thinking to the higher plane, and to understand and accept that our relationship would continue on the spiritual level where Chris was now free of pain and suffering and was experiencing joy and love beyond our comprehension.

This new understanding calmed my spirit, gave me a sense of peace, and helped me to accept my life as it now was. I was grieving not only the loss of my son but the loss of my close friend as well. But I was learning that I was walking the path that was intended for me, for Chris, and for our family. I was conscious that we were in God's loving presence. God saw our suffering and heartache and He was there with us, loved us, and understood our pain. He would not take away the trials through which we would learn, but He would bring us to greater understanding of the meaning of our lives. As painful as it was and would continue to be, He was leading us in the direction our lives were meant to take.

As I began to adjust to living without Chris, I understood and accepted that grief and sorrow had become a natural part of our lives. We could not change that, but we would be changed by it, just as we had been changed by and through Chris's illness. We had to continue to trust in the hand of God in our lives.

I continued to reflect on this gift and message from Chris. Perhaps the reason I had been selected to receive his message was because he and I were so closely bonded that I would be open to receiving it. But, this affirmation of what we believed was a gift for all of us. Chris would want each of us to know that love continues to flow between us; he would continue to participate in our lives and would hear us when we spoke to him. After Mass, I went home and related my beautiful experience to Jack and our children.

Four days later, Michele, John, and Maryann received an affirming letter from Deacon Ray Gartner, friend and former teacher, in which he shared his own experience when his parents died in an automobile accident. With his permission, part of the letter follows:

"The difficult road ahead is to dispel our emotions and allow him (Chris) to touch us in ways we can recognize, to let us know he is safe and at peace. I guess I became more convinced from the resurrection stories and from life, that those whom we love and have loved us do desire that. Our Lord himself desired very deeply to appear to His closest friends to tell them not to fear. And He did in ways they would recognize – in his manner of speaking, in the breaking of bread. This is what faith is about. It helps us, even in darkness to have the courage to turn anger, guilt, and grief into productive energy for Him."

I fully agree with Deacon Ray that those who loved us and have died do want to reach us to tell us not to fear, as Chris did the day of his burial and in many ways and on many occasions has continued to do since his death.

The trauma of losing Chris had made them apprehensive that another of us would get sick and die. Our children, realizing that Jack and I had been under great emotional and physical stress, urged us to take a trip, but we had no energy or enthusiasm to plan one. Finally, we managed to plan a trip out west by train, because it would be a slower transition than flying, thereby providing privacy and time to grieve and to heal while gradually adjusting to the idea of a vacation.

Journal Entry • June 7, 1987

I write this as I sit on Amtrak's California Zephyr, as it returns to Chicago after a trip that our children urged us to take. I've not been able to journal or to write about Chris's death until now, because the pain has been unbearable. I've needed time to be with Jack and the kids - to nurture and be nurtured by them. To simply learn to live with the pain and with life as it is.

My thoughts always go to Chris. I don't experience this as an intrusion. I want to think of him, to be in his presence. It comforts and consoles me to feel him around me. But the sorrow is overwhelming because I miss him so much.

My mind reels remembering the day he died — John and Michele arriving too late to see Chris a final time, John's pain and loss released in a torrent of tears that shook the three of us at we stood hugging in the doorway. Speaking with family and friends but mentally being with Chris: it's time to help Chris to turn, it's time to sit with Chris and visit, it's time for his medications. I felt as if I had come back from a long, arduous journey to a distant place and I had not been prepared for the transition. This place to which I had returned seemed strange and worst of all I was without purpose.

How grateful I am to Jack, my rock for his dependable, steady, loving presence throughout Chris's illness allowing only the demands of his practice to take him away from us. We had been of one mind: to be there physically, spiritually, and emotionally for Chris.

That evening, Michele, Maryann, and John, reminding us that we hadn't slept the night before, led us to our bedroom, sat with us as we spoke of Chris, and kissed us goodnight. Jack's first words to me the next morning, "Good morning, mother of a saint. Chris's first request of Jesus must have been, 'Please Jesus, give my parents their first good sleep in fifteen months.'" I remember, a few minutes later, a radiant Michele coming in to relate her healing dream of Christopher happily speaking with Einstein.

After Bill took Chris, I remember entering the living room to find Vicki consoling a sobbing Debbie who was to begin her shift at 7 a.m. Vicki reminded me that months ago, when she said, "This must be hard on you and Dr. Luce, I had replied, "No matter how hard it is on us, it's so much harder on Chris. He is giving us the courage to endure." Debbie added that Chris, Jack and I showed the nurses how to be strong. Ultimately, it was Chris who set the bar for all of us.

My waking thoughts are filled with fragments of the last months, days, hours, moments, parts of conversations, statements he made, memories of his childhood, Chris walking, Chris talking enthusiastically, Chris in pain, Chris dying. The pain I feel is so real it is physical – a heaviness in my abdomen, a squeezing in my brain, overwhelming grief that permeates my whole being. There is no remedy for death. It's done! Final! I will not see him again as he was, – Christopher – and all he meant to me.

My communication and connection to him is now strictly on the spiritual plane. He has another body now, one not subject to illness and pain. (Years later I learned that it is called the etheric body.) I believe he can go instantly to wherever he chooses, and when I talk to him, I know that he hears and understands me. And best of all he continues to love, to learn, to grow in knowledge.

All of us talk to him frequently. The first few days, I was fearful that my conversations with him would be intrusive, would prevent him from "doing" other things - wonderful, new, exciting things. I even told Chris he was free not to listen to me if it was intrusive. Now I think that in his more perfect state he is able to do many things at once, so I feel okay talking to him as much as I do.

Oh! How I miss Chris. I remember the things he loved: playing golf, walking in the woods, smelling the fresh air and the earth, walking in deep snow and feeling the cold on his face, taking pic-

tures of nature. Chris eagerly following John like his shadow to the baseball field, the pool, and the golf course. Sweet memories of the good years.

I have a beautiful memory of a perfect summer evening — the summer before our lives fell apart. Chris was on summer break from Purdue. His life had become all that he had dreamed it could be. He had several good friends in the fraternity; he had been elected house manager; he was dating again; and taking stimulating courses. That summer he was the happiest that I had seen him. He was enthusiastic about his future. With hands in his pockets, too animated to sit still, he would pace back and forth talking rapidly about the world of possibilities that lay ahead. He exuded excitement and vitality.

That summer evening Chris, Jack, and I took our boat out on Lake Michigan an hour before sunset. Chris was always with friends in the evenings, so it was a pleasant surprise when he said he would come with us. At the boat slip, Chris took the wheel, handling the boat with the same skill that was evident with most things that he did. With ease he maneuvered it out of the slip and into the channel keeping the power down so as not to create a wake. Then he turned the boat into the lake and slowly headed west toward the sunset and the National Park, Mount Baldy.

The water was calm and glassy, shimmering with a million pinpoints of reflected sunlight. The temperature was perfect with just a light gentle breeze, caused by the slow movement of the boat. From the shore came the sound of a soft ballad as picnickers enjoyed a late supper. Chris cut the engine and we quietly floated along listening to the music as the sky turned a burnished gold and the sun became an enormous, brilliant, orange-red ball. As the sun slipped below the horizon, the sky transformed itself into variegated shades of radiant pinks and soft apricots. We were surrounded by color as though the spectacle was just for us. We talked softly, comfortably, enjoying each other's company, in harmony with ourselves and with the universe. I recognized it as a perfect moment to be treasured and remembered for the rest of my life. A time capsule – our small boat, Jack and I and our son, innocent and content, floating on the golden shimmering water as loving energy surrounded and filled us; as though the universe wanted us to have a gift before the suffering that would change our lives began.

So many memories! So many images! At four, getting his first golf lesson and attacking the ball so hard he did a 360- degree turn and collapsing. As a preschooler, developing a loud voice so that his brother and sisters would pay attention to what he was saying. Watching a little six year old carefully carry his gold fish to the edge of the pond, gently drop it in, then brush away a tear from each eye as he said good-by. A dinner during a family vacation where eight-year-old Chris asked me to dance even though no one else was dancing and having other diners applaud as our dance ended. Chris, at nine picking up police signals from heaven knows where, because he had taped wires all over his bedroom windows and connected them to a large battery. At ten, with John's help, doing the electrical wiring for their model trains. Watching the two of them with their heads bent over the train table, earnestly discussing train layouts. At sixteen, winning the Junior Golf tournament at our club. In high school, winning a MVP award in golf. Chris walking into the mud-room and slamming the door shut. Chris sneaking up behind me and shouting "boo!" Chris in deep concentration loving whatever he was doing at the moment. Chris looking handsome in his tux going to his first prom. The way Chris addressed John – always saying his name twice – "John! John!" Chris, the photographer walking around with his camera slung around his neck taking pictures of school sports events, sunsets and snowstorms. Chris with both hands in his pocket, a smile on his face, animatedly telling jokes. Watching Chris's expressive eyes as he enthusiastically put forth his point of view. Watching those same eyes become sad, frightened, and filled with pain as the cancer spread through his spine. Looking into his eyes as he said, "Mom, I love you." "Mom, I can't begin to thank you for taking care of me." Sitting next to his bed in the family room watching him grow thinner and sicker. Jack and I on each side of Chris's bed our arms around him, gently talking to him as he labored through the last hours of his life here on earth - his eyes never leaving my face during those long hours. How still his body became after he drew his last breathe!

Terese Fabbri called him teacher! He was for me, for all of our family. He touched so many other people. Will his impact be greater because he died? Was that why he died? Instrument? I am so touched and awed by his visit on the night that he was buried. My beautiful son – his act of love affirming that our love and connection to each other will continue. I love Chris as he is now. I know he loves me more now because he is capable of more love. My guide, my friend, my teacher, and my protector.

Journal Entry • June 15, 1987

The last two days have been torture. Yesterday, Sunday, I felt a need to start taking care of Chris's room. As I entered the full impact of his personality, who he was and is overpowered me. I felt his presence in his room, in his things - his energy swirling around me - his likes, loves, hopes, dreams were all there - his interrupted hopes and dreams, and mine. The pain of losing him was unbearable. I felt the shock of his death as though for the first time. The finality made me light-headed and faint. I was over-whelmed with the longing to see him, to have him amidst all those belongings, and possessions which he held dear. I asked him to guide me and to be there with me because it was going to be a heartbreaking task.

He was a saver – always thinking of the future. Through the things that meant something to him, I learned more about my son. There were his treasures: his boy-scout hat, game ticket stubs, theater tickets, birthday cards, collections, books, camera equip-ment, medals, awards, report cards, and dozens of pictures that he had taken, posters, clay tiles and pots he had made in art class at Wabash, pictures of Ann, gifts she had given him. The memories of happy events made Chris real and present. I so desperately miss him.

As I carefully went through his clothes I realized I could not let go of everything. I saved his favorite sweaters and blazer, and one pair of shoes - symbols of Chris when he was healthy and free to walk and drive and live life fully. Perhaps later I will be able to give them away. But not now!

Oh Chris, how I need you here with me – I miss you. I want you to be able to live out your dreams. I feel depression in every cell of my body!

Journal Entry • June 18, 1987

Jack and I and John met Mark Gordon for lunch in Chicago. He was Chris's good friend and fraternity brother at Purdue. For me it was, if not a closure, at least an opportunity to tell Mark how much Chris appreciated his friendship. I told him he was remarkably loving and mature for a young man because he was able to work through his own pain in order to be a friend to Chris. (I had the opportunity to tell his mother the same thing a year later when Jack and I attended Mark's wedding.) Although many others called Chris at home, Mark was the one who called at least once a week and made Chris aware that he could handle whatever Chris wanted to share with him, and Chris loved and respected him for that.

The lunch gave us the opportunity to thank Mark for his part in the burial service. When Jack called Mark to tell him that Chris had died, Mark asked if Phi Kappa Psi fraternity could hold a service at the gravesite, and could we put Chris's fraternity pin on his lapel. We readily agreed to the ceremony but we were unable to locate the fraternity pin. At the wake when we told Mark we were unable to find the pin, Mark put his own pin on Chris. During lunch we thanked Mark for giving Chris his pin and promised to send him Chris's when we found it. A week later I found Chris's pin and sent it on to Mark knowing that it held special meaning for him.

Mark gave us pictures of Chris that had been taken at the

spring and Christmas fraternity dances. We treasure them. Mark said Chris, even though he was a transfer student, fit into the fraternity immediately and the guys really liked him. At the wake, Eric had told us that Chris would have been elected house president. How Chris would have loved that.

I sat there during lunch barely able to hold back the tears. I kept thinking that we were having lunch with Chris's friend and Chris should have been there too. But Chris wasn't there and never would be. It was good to be with Mark so that we could thank him personally; but oh how hard it was to ask him about his job, to know he has a girlfriend, an apartment, a future. He would get married and have children. I was happy for Mark. And I so want the same for Chris. It is the right order of things. Twenty three-year-old men should have futures. I pine for Chris.

I am so emotionally unstable. I never know when I will cry. Sometimes I'm fine. I smile, even laugh, have dinner with friends. But sometimes, now, I feel hollow, physically weak. Eternal crying!

The Fall after Chris's death we received a call from Mark inviting our family to attend a ceremony in memory of Chris at the Phi Kappa Psi fraternity house in Lafayette. It would take place during Homecoming weekend when Mark's class and Chris's friends could be present. Mark explained to us that Chris's fraternity brothers wanted to mark Chris's passing with a memorial that would last through the years. They had decided they wanted the memorial to be a small block of granite.

The beautiful ceremony was held on the grounds of the fraternity house. Our family, the fraternity brothers and Gordon Sheffield, Chris's roommate from Wabash gathered around the granite marker which had been inscribed with Chris's name, dates of birth and death and a Latin phrase, Amici Usque Adaras, - among loving friends. The inscription was the same as the one on the plaque that had been given to us by the fraternity after the gravesite ceremony. Two burning bushes flanked the stone.

Mark spoke of how Chris had touched their lives, how much

he had loved Phi Kappa Psi fraternity, and how diligently he had worked for the fraternity during the short time he was there. I also spoke - grateful for the opportunity to tell Chris's fraternity brothers how much their friendship and the life in the fraternity had meant to him - truly a high point in his life. I assured them that they had gifted him as much as he had gifted them and thanked them on behalf of Chris and our family for the beautiful tribute to his memory.

I also told them of a dream that Chris had had in the early spring before his death. As I stood listening to Mark, I recalled the dream that Chris had related to me. He had dreamt that he was hovering above the grounds of the fraternity house while a ceremony was being held outdoors. Even the location of the ceremony in the dream was the same as the site where we were now standing. Neither Chris nor I knew what the dream meant. In my remarks I shared all this and told them that I believed that Chris's dream was a foreshadowing of this ceremony, and perhaps Christopher was not as far away as we thought. During the luncheon that followed we presented the fraternity with a much-needed projector and personally thanked the friends who had meant so much to our son.

Journal Entry • June 19, 1987

What do I do for my son now? I visit him at the cemetery and place both hands flat on the grass above his face because that is the closest I can get to him. I pull a dead blossom from a pot of geraniums. We are in the process of choosing a headstone for the grave that looks so bleak. Two panels of fresh sod mark the cut out made for the casket. I can visualize what he looked like, what he was wearing, the crucifix in his hand, his ring, the fraternity pin on his lapel. I visualize the clothes that John selected for his brother: Chris's favorite gray suit, his favorite tie, argyle socks I had knitted, and his new loafers.

Yesterday, Terese gave me a tape of "On Eagles Wings" that she had made for Michele. John and I played it and cried because it brought back vivid memories of the Funeral Mass. Such beautiful words "He will raise you up on eagle's wings!"

I want him back! He's been gone long enough! I want him back! Whole! Happy! Driving up in his car, walking in through the garage door. I want to hear the characteristic noise of the door slamming behind him, so that I know that it is Chris that has just come in. I can almost hear his firm, strong steps on the tiles as he walks through the kitchen.

Memories! How precious! I know Chris is watching me now, observing my loss, my pain. I imagine him wanting to console me, trying to tell me he is fine, to remind me of my own words to him, "Chris, I want you to know that I will know where you are." I know he is happy now, wonderfully fulfilled, loving, doing, learning. For him there is joy. For him I can rejoice. He has the prize - continuation of life on a higher plane.

In June, after Chris's death, Maryann and Dave moved to our area. Maryann was postponing the completion of her residency until after their children were in school and Dave, having completed his residency and fellowship, was ready to start a practice.

It was so good to have them living near us, not only for Jack and me, but for Maryann as well. Throughout the course of Chris's illness, Maryann had felt the isolation that came from living one hundred and fifty miles away. Her daily calls to us were filled with longing and the need to be with us. Within twenty months, she had given birth to two children, lost her brother, and had thyroid surgery. All of the family's energy had gone into caring for Chris. She had to care for two infants and deal with the impending loss of her brother while living two States away.

It was great consolation that now they were living five minutes away from us. Little David and Nicole made us laugh at a time when we thought we would never even smile again; and for a few minutes at a time, we forgot how sad we were. John

and Michele came often because we all needed the comfort and
security that being together in one room brought to all of us.

When Chris became ill John, Michele, Maryann and Dave
became more thoughtful and selfless not only toward Chris, but
also toward one another. After Chris died this spirit of concern
and love continued as they drew strength from each other and
valued their time together. But as good as it was to be together,
we all felt Chris's absence and the large hole in our lives.

Journal Entry • September 25, 1987, 5:56 a.m.

*Hi Chris. I awoke very early again. Coming downstairs to think
or to write is better than trying to get back to sleep. I am aware of
you so often. Now, this moment, I feel your presence. I know you
hear me and love me. This month has been so hard, as will the
coming months and years. I am re-living last year almost day by
day. My mind floods with heart breaking scenes and memories,
then your pain and mine become real again. I look at the garden
and it reminds me of you. I walk past your room and stop to look
in, but you're not there. Your notebook remains in the corner of
the family room hearth, because it's comforting to have it there – a
reminder of you!*

*I feel your presence all around me. You are never far from my
conscious thoughts. I try to stay connected to you, my son, my
friend, spirit. I feel sorrow because I cannot see and hug you, hear
your step, hear your wonderful voice, and enjoy conversations
with you. These are my losses. Because I cannot change anything,
I reluctantly admit and accept them. But I try to focus on your
life now which I perceive as completely fulfilling, and that allevi-
ates some of my sorrow. I relive your loving visit the evening of
the day you were buried and I am consoled. Each day I wish you
a happy birthday – your birth into your new life. Your last birthday on earth was so sad; it comforts me to say, "Happy Birthday
in Jesus, Chris."*

What is life like for you? You don't sleep, or feel pain; there are no days or nights. Right? You can do several things at once and you can be in several places at once. You can hear me, Dad, John, Michele, Maryann. We probably often talk to you at the same time, don't we? I don't think that our talking to you interferes with your life since you can do many things at once. I think you have access to a vast body of knowledge and truth now; and you can learn as quickly as you are capable of doing. Oh! Knowing how much you love to learn, that must make you very happy. I think you want to tell me that all your earthly suffering was nothing or at least worth it to have attained what you have now. Just as a woman forgets the pain of childbirth when she feels the joy of holding her newborn, so it is with you. Oh! I'm so happy to know you are experiencing such joy.

Can you "zap" yourself anywhere you want to go? Anywhere? Do you study? Talk to the great minds like Einstein, St. Thomas? What is Jesus like? Have you met Dad's father, your grandmothers? Have you special friends? What is a "day" like? For that matter, what is a "moment" like? But I forget there is no time as we know it, only the eternal present, the eternal Now. Do you have different "activities", a home, responsibilities? Can you see us all the time or only when we talk to you? Do you visit our home, the family room, your room, the train room, the garden? Do you whisper in my ear and give me direction? I think that you do. I love you. Pray for us! I pray for you!

Journal Entry • October 5, 1987

Five months ago today, Chris, you passed on to eternal life with Jesus. I rejoice with you and for us, because you are there and are showing us the way. I feel so open to you and to the world of spirit. Through my connectedness with you, I also can share in this world. Our connection is my vehicle to your new enlightened world. As I think about your new life, I experience, gradually, an awareness of what it must be like to be on the other side. I experience you as free, as having great freedom to move instantly from anywhere to anywhere. You can hear and see me writing to you, hear all of us that love you, while also participating in many other things. I think you experience other planets, immense bodies of knowledge, truth, great, great love, intense joy. You are more understanding, more compassionate, and wiser. You have an incredible capacity for love.

Your death and rebirth in the new life have opened up a new way of thinking. It has expanded my sense of the spirit and spiritual world. The curtain still divides us, but it seems sheerer now. I see glimmers. I have a better awareness. Part of me is there with you. I feel connected with you, as though your spirit surrounds me wherever I go. I love it! Your presence sustains me so that I'm able to participate in life, grow, share, and love. I have not shut down to living because life is too important to waste. I know how much you wanted to live so you could fulfill your dreams. But your soul had other plans. I know that if I waste my life, you will be disappointed in me. You wanted me to go on living. Before you died, you said, "I don't want you to mope around like Jim's mother did after he died. Get on with your life. This family has too much talent to have it go to waste." I am trying to move on, we all are, one step at a time, Chris.

I miss you – sharing thoughts, ideas, and hopes with you, seeing and listening to you. I feel sadness so deep and intrinsic – it will forever be a part of me. Yet, I am aware that physical reality is merely a small part of our lives and of reality itself. Your presence in the family room on the evening of the day your body was buried affirms in the most loving way that you and so, we, are more than our physical bodies. Our spirits continue to grow, and to love, and to care for those that we loved in this life.

When you interrupted my thoughts with your message that there is no separation between us, I know you were affirming what we had talked about before you died. And you were saying, "Yes, Mom, we are still connected because love doesn't end when we die." Thank you, Chris, for coming to tell me.

Chris, I recently reread all the beautiful cards and notes that were sent to us after your death. I again was so moved by the love and compassion extended in the written messages. You touched many people, you know. But Chris, several of the condolence cards had messages printed by the card company that stated that our loved one would live on because of our wonderful memories of him. I drew little comfort from these messages because they seemed inaccurate. Finally, I realized what it was that sounded false. There was no belief in life after death. Chris, I believe that you and all who die live on whether or not we hold you in our memories. One has nothing to do with the other. You live on because your spirit – your soul is eternal; and even if every single one of us stopped thinking of you and never thought of you again, you would still be alive because your spirit, the nonphysical part of you will never die.

Honey, in the weeks and months since your death, I have spent long periods of time reflecting on your new life. In the condolence cards that I reread - the term, "May he rest in peace" is often used. What does that mean? In human terms, it can narrowly be defined as quiet tranquil repose. I've reasoned that the term only sounds great if one is referring to the death of an old person who has had a long life Then resting in peace sounds like a reward doesn't it? However, would God call you, a twenty-three year old to heaven or my two-year-old my sister, so that you could have quiet tranquil repose?

I think that life in the spirit has to be much more than that. I believe that peace is a quality of your spirit now. Being at peace is the state of your soul and I don't think it refers to passivity or dormancy, but rather to tranquility and harmony. I visualize your spirit as being more fully alive than it ever was here on earth. Being at peace is the condition of your beautiful soul, as it grows in all aspects of love. I celebrate your growth.

I feel a peacefulness that comes from knowing that I am in truth. Each of us learns the same things but in different ways. I've learned so much about life and about the next life from you – from loving and caring for you, from sharing your pain, from being there for each other day after day. In letting go of you, I've been able to continue to experience you and your love for me and for all of us.

In the last twenty-four hours, I seem to be aware of an atmosphere of love in this house- like oxygen – it's everywhere in this house. I feel it is you. In spite of all the merger problems Dad is experiencing and bringing home to discuss, I feel this sense of, what should I call it? Is it serenity? Love?

This morning, after coming home from a Mass for you at St. Anthony Hospital Chapel, I watched a program about the Hopi Indians. How beautifully simple their life is, how attuned to nature. They are devoid of pretense and have no need to accumulate material possessions. They respect the life spirit found in all things. I too, want to let go of material things. It's time! Chris, I love you. May Jesus keep you in the palm of his hand.

In the months following Chris's death, I struggled on many levels to deal with his death. On one level I understood that Chris died on May 5th because his work on this earth was completed and God was calling him to participate in another, higher life in the spirit. On a human level, I missed him very much. I missed his presence, his ideas, his voice. On another level, I felt I had failed as a mother because I had not been able to keep our son alive. Mothers protect their children - keep them from harm. Where had I failed? What had I not done?

I replayed the past year and one-half almost day by day. I replayed past events all the way back to before I knew that I was pregnant with Christopher and took medication to alleviate gall bladder attacks. Although I stopped the medication when I learned I was pregnant; I had always feared that what I had taken might have harmed his immune system.

I searched for reasons why he had gotten cancer. Was it due to his early allergy to fat? Was it caused by an environmental factor? Could the cause have been toxic fertilizers on the golf course where he had spent so much time playing golf? Was it due to a toxic waste sight located within the city limits? Had the grief he felt over breaking up with his girlfriend lowered his immune system? Was it due to a hereditary factor?

I felt emotionally depleted. I went through the motions, but I was an outsider, an observer, rather than a participant in life. I knew I had to pick up the threads of my life. I remembered Chris's hope that after his death I would not drop out of life. With that thought in mind, I made myself enroll in the second summer semester at IUSB in order to complete the remaining eighteen hours of the master's program.

I returned to school feeling displaced and disoriented. I had been on another planet where courses of study, grades, and course requirements were unimportant. For over a year, I had been with Chris in hospital rooms and in our family room. Although each day was emotionally and physically stressful, it was where I wanted to be - nothing else was important. When Chris died, I felt abandoned. Nothing would ever be as meaningful and important as taking care of him, consequently, it was difficult to begin living a normal life again where I could focus on everyday events, study, and plan for the future.

Jack and our children, who had not been able to simply drop out of life when Chris became ill, were able to integrate quicker than I. I went through the summer and fall as two people. Therese, the student went through the motions of going to class, studying, completing assignments, while Therese, the mother continued to attend Mass each day, mourn, and experience loss and emptiness. I wondered what I was doing back in school. The whole effort seemed meaningless to me; but I persisted because I knew Chris wanted me too and I knew that over time, I would be glad that I did.

During those months I began to address my anger toward Dr. Smith. I felt a strong desire to forgive the past and everyone in it. The call to forgive seemed to be in stereophonic sound, because I was hearing the same message from many sources – from books I was reading, from dreams, from homilies during

Mass, and finally from my heart. I wanted to let go of my anger and simply grieve for Chris. In retrospect, I realize that forgiving Dr. Smith came in small increments over time. Even though I made an act of the will to forgive him, whenever I saw him I froze, barely able to speak. Jack, who saw him at the hospital several times a week, was able to forgive quicker than I. It took nine years for me to completely forgive him. It happened finally when I invited him to Jack's retirement party. When he arrived I hugged him, and I really meant it when I thanked him for coming. As I hugged him I heard him whisper, "Finally." I knew that he understood that at last I had truly forgiven him.

The one thing that had meaning and gave me a sense of purpose was writing about our last months with Christopher. I was filled with sorrow, raw emotions and heartbreaking memories –and writing seemed to drain off and alleviate the pain. But grief, that up, down, around, and sideways roller coaster of emotions was now a part of my life. I could not pretend that the worst experience in my life never happened. I had to grieve for Chris.

Gradually, as spring approached, I began to feel a sense of integration. But the grieving process would go on for years. Grief was mitigated by the knowledge that Chris was no longer suffering and loving his new life. If I could have lifted the veil that separates us from the next life I would have; because I had a burning desire to know what Chris was experiencing now that he had made the transition to the next life.

❧ 10 ❧

SIGNS AND VISITS – GOODBYE IS NOT FOREVER

We never lose the ones we love who have made the transition to the next life. I am convinced of this, because in the seventeen years since his death, we have had many experiences through which I learned that Chris is still with us and wishes us to be aware of his continued love and concern for us.

Perhaps having contact with a loved one who has died is not such an unusual experience. It could be that, like near-death experiences, no one spoke of them until recently. But, I believe, they have always occurred. In 1915, at eight years of age, my mother had an experience that she vividly recalls. To this day, at the age of ninety-seven, she maintains that "I saw heaven. It was not a dream."

It wasn't until I read Moody and Kubler-Ross that I identified the experience my mother had as NDE, near-death experience. Many people have had near-death experiences, but until recently no one spoke of them. Like NDE, I believe that many people have been touched by deceased loved ones but do not speak of it. Perhaps then, by openly sharing our experiences, others will be encouraged to share theirs.

From my own and my family's experiences and from the literature, it seems that those who have made the transition are able to support those whom they cared for in this life. Writers like Altea, Puryear, Moody, Kubler-Ross, and Van Praagh validate our experiences. Information from NDE accounts, indicate that we continue to learn and to grow in love after we die, suggesting that our souls are in a process of growing and evolving. NDE experiencers affirm over and over again that life on the human plane is only an interim in our eternal life as spirits. Perhaps then, having contact with those they have left behind is simply a

continuation of love and the process of growth. The good news
of the Gospels affirmed in the present day in a concrete way
through the generosity of our God who loves us so much!

I have had several powerful experiences. Each one has
increased my belief that life after death is incredibly exciting.
My experience on the evening of the day Chris was buried confirmed what I had told him while he was ill: that love continues
because there is no separation after death. God allowed Chris
to bring this message when I needed him, as though he had
been waiting for the right moment to reach me. That experience was important coming when it did on the day that he was
buried. The memory of it sustained and nurtured me as I slowly and painfully felt my way and emerged from the experience
of caring for, and letting go of Chris's earthly being. God
reminded me that He was there to support me, revealing truths
beyond my knowledge, and helping me to be more aware of the
world of spirit and its infinite possibilities.

Reflecting on the gift that I received that evening I know that
the message is meant for everyone. God loves us profoundly
and He wishes to ease our anguish and fear that when our loved
ones die, they are lost to us. He wants us to know that they are
still with us and continue to love us, nurture us, and pray for
our well-being.

Five incredible occurrences that I believe were all connected
began in January of 1994 and continued over a period of six
months. They were a further confirmation that Chris was able
to participate in our lives and I believe that he also wanted us to
stop grieving and to fully celebrate his new life.

A renewed interest in angels had taken place and many books
were available. The previous fall, I had read two books that
were accounts of people who had had unusual experiences they
could only explain as the work of angels. I didn't dwell on the
stories, but I had read them and they now were a part of my
own understanding and memory. Looking back I believe that
my interest in angels was not an accident. Sometimes God pro-

vides opportunities that prepare us to understand and accept future events. There are no accidents as Jean Houston says, "This is not a random universe;" there is a definite plan that is always at work in our lives.

I will begin by relating that on a cold, snowy Saturday in January of 1994, Jack was in a serious auto accident in which his car was demolished. He was broad-sided by a driver, who because of the steep slope and icy road conditions lost control and slammed into Jack's car driving it into a short wall. Had he been at the scene one second sooner he would have been seriously injured or killed. As it was, the air bag deployed and thankfully he walked away with only a stiff neck and bruises on his forehead and knee. Was it a lucky break or was an angel at work?

Three days later, on Tuesday morning, I started out for the hospital where I worked as the director of a program. It was 6:45 a.m. and fairly dark. The streets were covered with snow that had frozen into uneven tracks of ice and driving was hazardous. I drove down Springland Avenue past the place where Jack had had his accident three days earlier and turned into Vail Street - a narrow two lane residential street with curbs. Due to many resurfacings, the pavement is crowned causing the center of the street to be higher than the sides. It's not an easy street to drive even when the weather is good.

As I turned into Vail Street and drove a few feet, the car began to skid on the icy street. Just then my headlights picked up three teenagers dressed in dark clothing walking three abreast on the street a few feet ahead of me. I saw only their backs. They must have heard the car and noticed the headlights, because they all turned around and looked at me as the car skidded toward them. Then, instead of stepping off the street or walking single file to get out of my way, they again turned their backs to me and continued to walk three abreast on the right side of the street.

I was driving slowly, but even so I could not come to a complete stop, because I was afraid if I applied too much pressure on the brake I would lose control of the car. I knew I would hit the boys unless I turned away from them and headed into the oncoming lane. But a car was approaching in that lane. The narrow, two lane street allowed no room to avoid both the boys and the car. The boys continued to walk three abreast ahead of me on the right side of the street. The car coming toward me was not slowing down even though the driver must have seen my predicament.

I did not want to hit the boys. I quickly made my decision to head into the left lane toward the oncoming car which was now only a few feet away. I purposely headed toward the headlights of the oncoming car knowing that in a moment I was going to be in an accident that I had caused. As I aimed toward the car I must have shut my eyes waiting for the impact. Then, a split second later, I felt the movement of the wheel in my hands as though someone had turned the wheel. Seconds must have gone by as I waited for impact. But there was no impact. My eyes flew open and I saw that I was passing the car with only inches to spare and I had not hit the boys. They were behind me still walking three abreast on the right side of the street.

I was stunned. I didn't know how I had avoided hitting the car. Had an angel turned the wheel? I knew I hadn't. I had made the decision to hit the car. With my eyes shut and no room to maneuver I could not have adjusted the wheel myself.

Looking back, it seems as though I was the only one having a crisis. The boys saw me but didn't get off the street. They just kept walking ahead of me. The driver of the other car had to have seen my car swerving on the ice and the boys on the street, but didn't slow down or stop. Yet there was no accident and I couldn't explain why. I replayed the scene every day as I drove down Vail Street to the hospital. How had I avoided hitting the car and the boys? Had an angel saved all of us?

On a Monday evening, two weeks later, there were two more unusual occurrences. Jack had just left for the hospital to deliver a baby. Having finished in the kitchen around 6:45 pm,

I came into the family room where the television was on. I was looking forward to a program that would be airing at 7:00 p.m. Before sitting down, I went over to the fireplace hearth to straighten a stack of books. As I turned around the thought came to me that the room was filled with angels. I immediately wondered if Chris was one of them. I had never thought of the possibility that Chris could be an angel until that moment. It was a lovely, pleasant thought but merely that. I had already forgotten it as I settled down in my favorite chair absently staring at the TV, waiting for the 7:00 o'clock program to begin. Suddenly the TV set made a very loud noise and went dark. No sound! No picture! It was the same kind of sound that the earlier picture tubes made when they blew out. When that happened we knew we had to call the TV repair man because we would need a new picture tube. But we were well past the day of the old picture tube.

I sat there for a moment feeling disappointed that I wouldn't be able to watch my program. Then I remembered that I should turn off the power to the set. At least that's what we did in the Fifties when the tube blew out. Reluctantly, I pressed the remote's off button to turn off the power. To my surprise, the picture and sound immediately came on. There was nothing wrong - the picture was fine, as was the sound. Thinking we might have experienced a power outage, I called our friends across the street and asked if they had just lost power to their TV. They said no, they hadn't experienced any problems.

At that point I remembered my thought that the room was filled with angels and Chris might be one of them. Was Chris telling me that I was right; he was an angel now and he was right in this room? I recalled that when he was a teenager, Chris loved to sneak up behind me and yell boo and laugh when I jumped. Was this Chris again making a loud noise to get my attention? When I read James Van Praagh's book, _Talking To Heaven_, I knew that it could indeed have been Chris. Van Praagh explains that when spirits communicate with us they sometimes use electrical objects such as light switches, electric fans, and television sets to make their presence known.

I recounted my experience to Jack when he returned. The two of us shook our heads not knowing what to make of it and wondered if it was Chris. The next morning when I called Maryann to relate the strange incident to her she immediately asked me the time it had occurred. I told her between 6:50 p.m. and 7:00 p.m. She said, "Mom, I have goose bumps." She had had a strange experience at that same time. While rocking and breast-feeding Dominic in his room she heard what sounded like a baby, or an animal crying and a few seconds later a sound like wind whistling. The sounds were coming from an area of the ceiling where there are no windows. Not knowing what else to make of it she had a thought that it had been Chris trying to get her attention. We agreed that Chris must have visited both of us.

I read that when Jesus rose from the dead He only had to appear once to show that he had risen from the dead. However, he appeared many times to a number of people in order to confirm the first appearance and to reaffirm that he had truly risen. Could it be that Chris came to me to confirm his coming to Maryann? Or could he have come to Maryann to reinforce the TV incident and my thought that he is now an angel? Could this be? Could Chris have become an angel? Since then I've read many books on related topics. I believe now that it is possible for Chris to have become an angel or returned to being an angel because angels take on many forms.

In the spring and summer of 1994 I kept turning these events over in my mind. I continued to wonder if Chris had protected Jack from serious injury, and if he had saved me from hitting the boys or the oncoming car, caused the TV explosion, and the sounds that Maryann heard, and was he now an angel? Whenever I drove on Vail Street, I'd remember the strange and miraculous morning in January and wonder if it was an angel that had saved us and was the angel Chris.

In early July of that same year I was again driving down Vail Street. It was a sunny, summer day. As I passed the place where the incident had occurred, I again wondered if it was Chris who had protected me. Was he one of my guardian angels now? Was he still called Christopher?

Suddenly from behind I heard what sounded like a very noisy engine badly in need of a new muffler or a tune-up. The noise got my attention and I glanced in the rear view mirror and saw a red car. The car came up behind me, quickly passed me, and immediately cut in front of me. It was then that I saw a sign in the car's rear window that stunned me. I couldn't help but notice it because it was at least half as high as the window and almost as long nearly filling the rear window. It seemed to be firm but flexible and appeared to be of the same color and material as that of manila folders. There were nine large letters printed in black across the sign: C H R I S T O P H. I could not see if there were other letters because the end of the sign was folded over on itself.

I am almost never aware of signs in or on cars unless I'm stopped behind one at a stoplight. I was made aware of that car because of the noise it made even before it passed me and even though the car was moving, I couldn't miss the sign because it was so large.

Chris confirmed for me in no uncertain terms that he is an angel now. He does watch over us, and he wants us to know that. Was he an angel before he was born to us and became Christopher? I don't know that yet. Angel stories seem to indicate that angels can take on human form. I do know that through his illness and death he changed us.

I am so grateful to have had the sign experience and am overwhelmed by God's generosity in allowing Chris to respond in a very human, concrete manner. Further, if Chris could give me this sign just as I was thinking about him, he must be able to read my thoughts and respond to them.

Shortly after I saw the sign, Jack and I purchased a beautiful angel to symbolize Chris's new life. I stopped wondering who came to my aid on Vail Street, who protected Jack from serious injury, who "blew out" the TV set, and who made the crying sounds that Maryann heard. All the questions were answered when I saw the sign reading, CHRISTOPH.

There have been many other times when we believed that Chris was with us. Occasionally, a light will be on that neither Jack nor I have turned on; the overhead fan in the family room will turn on or increase in speed when neither Jack nor I have been near the switch. The television set will turn off. Michele has discovered her slippers neatly placed on the landing, the bedroom fan will turn on, at times the light in her bedroom will go on in the middle of the night.

Our fourteen year-old granddaughter, Jenna and I have separately experienced the sound of silverware repeatedly dropping into the sink – but the sink is empty. One Sunday morning Jenna, already late for Mass, was taking her time getting dressed when two CDs that were on top of her CD player went flying across the room. Terrified, she quickly dressed and dashed out to the car where her sister, Nicole was patiently waiting to drive them to Mass. Just then Jenna realized that she had forgotten something and ran back to the door that she had just closed, a door that is never locked. To her shock the door was locked from the inside. Was her Uncle Chris chiding her for not having her priorities straight?

One morning in 2000, Jack and I were sitting at the kitchen counter having coffee and reading the paper, when Michele called so agitated, she was stuttering. She said, "I need your help." She had quit her job and although she believed it was the right decision; she was nevertheless in turmoil worrying if she had done the right thing.

As I listened to her reasons for quitting I knew she was doing soul work. I told her that her spirit was telling her she had other work to do in her life. I commended her on her decision and continued talking to her about her apparent need to make changes in her life and move on.

As I was speaking the eight recessed lights in the kitchen and family room slowly dimmed and went out for a second. I exclaimed, "Oh My Gosh, Michele, Chris just affirmed what I said, Chris is here!" and told her about the lights. I had no doubt that it was Chris. In the meantime, Jack went to the other part of the house to see if the electric clocks were flashing as they would have in an actual power outage, but they were not. We knew it was Chris doing his best to communicate his approval of Michele's decision.

One early morning in February of 2001 I was ready to leave for Maryann's house to prepare breakfast and drive our grand-children to school. It was something I did while Maryann was doing her residency, because whenever Dave had an early morning procedure, he needed help getting everyone off to school. Jack and I were talking, standing a few feet from the door to the garage when suddenly we were startled by the sound of beeping coming from within the garage. We were so taken aback that even though we were only a few feet from the door, the horn beeped four or five times before Jack had the presence of mind to yank the door open to see what was going on. The van horn was beeping and the headlights were flashing. As we stood there gaping, the horn stopped beeping and the lights stopped flashing. Neither of us had been in the garage since the day before and the overhead door had been closed all night. No one had been around the car. We looked at each other, smiled, and agreed that it must have been Chris visiting and telling us he was near.

A month later, Jack and I left for a winter trip to Florida. I always pray that we have a safe trip and ask the Blessed Mother and our angels and guides to protect us during our two day drive. As usual, I told Chris we were going to Florida, and knowing how much he had loved that area of Florida, I invited him to accompany us if he could. It's my way of including him. Whenever we have holiday gatherings I invite him to be there if he can. This trip was no exception as I invited him to come along.

Before settling into the condo we rent each year, we stop to visit our friends in central Florida and spend the evening with them. When we arrived after a long two day drive, we pulled into the cul de sac in front of their home, turned off the ignition, locked the car, and walked to their front door where we hugged and greeted Lee and Evelyn whom we had not seen since the year before.

As we stood talking in the entry way, we were again startled by beeping coming from Jack's car. We turned in unison and saw that the lights were also flashing. The noise and the flashing were persistent and continued until Jack used his remote to open the car door which stopped the flashing and beeping. What could we say to our friends who looked bewildered, except the truth as we knew it. "Oh, that's Chris, he sometimes reminds us that he's with us." They still looked bewildered even after we told them some of the other occurrences. Who could blame them!

A year later, another trip to Florida and again I invited Chris to join us if he could. As usual we stopped to visit our friends and this time we pulled into the side driveway instead of parking on the street. We walked through the breezeway and into the kitchen, and had no sooner said hello when the car horn began to beep persistently and the lights started to flash. Again Jack reached for the remote to open the car door and everything stopped. And we again explained to our still bewildered and confused friends that it was Chris telling us, "I'm here – I have accompanied you and kept you safe as you asked."

The horn did not beep for another seven months. Then in early September when our friend was visiting it happened again. Jim is a priest who stays with us during the time that he gives his annual retreat in our area. We had asked him if he would say Mass at our home one morning during his visit and he had graciously agreed. It was raining on the morning he was to say Mass, so instead of having Mass on the deck, Jim, our friend

Maryann and Jack and I sat on the sofa in our living room.

It was a simple service with each of us participating in the beautiful prayers of the Liturgy. At the hand shake of peace, we stood and hugged one another wishing each other the peace of the Lord. At that very moment the car horn began to beep. The four of us jumped at the unexpected sound. In unison, Jack and I said, "It's Chris!" I am convinced that Chris wanted us all to know that he had joined us and he was extending to each of us the peace of the Lord. Jim and Maryann were astonished. Jim had tears in his eyes and kept exclaiming, "O My gosh!"

Maryann said, "I know you've told me about these incidences, but one has to really experience it. I'm a believer now." Both of them had known that Chris visits us, but it's one thing to hear something and another to experience it. It's difficult to find words to describe how grateful I am for the gift of Chris's presence and affirmation of his love.

A month later, during football season, Jack and I had ten of our friends over for a Sunday afternoon to watch the Bears play. The Bears had been losing so there was a lot of moaning and groaning coming from the family room. And then the Bears scored. Just then the car horn started beeping startling all twelve of us. Jack and I met at the garage door, smiled and agreed that Chris wanted us to know that he was cheering the Bears too. Jack, John, and Chris had always watched the Bears together through good times and bad. Maybe Chris is still a fan with a sense of humor!!!

I have reflected upon these five incidences. The first time, only Jack and I were present. The next four were at significant moments and when others were present. I have concluded that Chris wants others to know that our loved ones continue to participate in our lives after they make the transition to the next.

Other members of our family have also had experiences with Christopher which started soon after Chris died. Two events occurred in the spring, almost a year after Chris died, which affirmed my own experiences and emerging belief that Chris

was able to contact us. Michele and Jack's mother believed that
Chris had appeared to them.

My mother-in-law, Mary, recounted the following experience.
The incident happened a few nights before and she was still
very moved by it. It had occurred while she was asleep in the
living room. Due to repair work being done in her bedroom,
she had been sleeping on the sleeper sofa in the living room.
When she finished recounting the story, I asked her to repeat it
in order to record her exact words using a tape recorder. These,
then, are her exact words.

"I was sound asleep, facing the wall with my back to the
center of the room. All of a sudden, the whole area of the
room became bright, like lights went on. It sort of hurt my
eyes and I had to blink. I jumped when the whole area
became lit up. It was just all lit up. No lamp lights, but the
whole area was lit up. The light was brilliant, but it wasn't
white, white, it was golden white. I sat up right away, still
facing the wall. There was not a stick of furniture in the
room. Nothing! Nothing! (In actuality the room is filled
with furniture including a piano) I was fully conscious; it
was not a dream. I didn't even know what I was sitting on,
but I was in a sitting position.

I was staring and frightened because of the light. I wondered what was happening. I didn't move until something
made me. Then it seemed like something was making me
turn around. I looked over my shoulder so I was facing
into the room, and there was Christopher standing very
tall. He was all in white. He was wearing a suit with a
jacket. His suit wasn't a white white, it was a golden, brilliant white. He was standing with his arms down and to
the side with his palms out and with a frown on his face.
And then all of a sudden, his face brightened up, and he
smiled and brought his arms up and brought his hands
closer together.

And then all of a sudden, everything disappeared, and I

was in the room just the way it is. I was sitting on the bed. Boy! Did I jump out of bed. I said, 'My God, what's happening?' I turned on a floor lamp and sat in a chair and said the rosary. Afterwards, I felt like the whole world came off my shoulders. What a relief! A relief about what? I don't know!

Then, when I got up in the morning, his picture, frame and all, was there on the floor where he had been standing. How on earth did that get there? His picture had been on the wall in a frame held with little picture hooks. Now it was on the floor face up. I had not seen it when I got up and said the rosary.

Another thing, I can't sit up unless I struggle this way and that way. I have to wiggle and twist. But no, I just sat right up, just like that! No problem!

Therese, I have a confession to make. I was upset and angry because I couldn't come to see Chris. I'm his grandmother. I felt mad because I didn't get to see him. But I never said anything. I said, 'if that's the way it is to be, help me to accept it.'

I think Chris was displeased with me! He was scolding me. Why didn't I accept things the way he wanted them? He didn't want me to come to see him. He didn't say anything. It was just the expression on his face, a frown, as though he was upset with me. When it finally dawned on me what he was trying to tell me, I thought, 'Okay Chris, I'm sorry.' Then his face broke out in a smile, and then he brought his hands together and lifted them up. I felt that he was embracing me. I think he was trying to tell me that it was all right. He had wanted to spare me. He didn't want me to worry about him or to be concerned about him, and I'm sure he knew how much I loved him. He was a very private person. But everyone knew that he loved everyone because he was that kind of a person.

But, oh! Therese, I don't think I'll ever be able to explain the light. I guess heaven has to be like that. No furniture, nothing. Everybody being able to go wherever they wish. I'm glad he told me. I feel close to him all the time. I think he loves me, and I think he is watching over me."

The following is an account of Michele's experience. It took place on May 13, 1988, a year after Chris died. These are Michele's exact words.

"On two occasions since my brother's death, I have seen Christopher. He has appeared to me. The first was on the night that he died. In my sleep he appeared to me. He was dressed in blue, and I only saw the top half of his body. He was very, very happy, and he was talking to Einstein. I knew by seeing his face that he was at peace and that he was happy.

The second time he appeared to me was on May 13, 1988. I was at my desk at work, and I was very sad. I closed my eyes, and he was right there. He was dressed in white and around him was the most bright, bright, intense white light. It was like looking into the sun but it didn't hurt your eyes, and he was just so beautiful and happy. He was wearing a casual white shirt. It was kind of buttoned down, and he was wearing white casual pants and white shoes like deck shoes. And he came over to me and he hugged me and I was able to hug him back. And that was very important to me. During the course of his illness, I couldn't hug him and I wanted to, and I was allowed to do that. (Chris's spine was very fragile due to the tumor spreading through his spine, consequently we couldn't hug him).

I think the significance of his appearing to me is that he knew how much I loved him. He knew I cared about his happiness, and it was his way of letting me know that he was okay and that he was happy. But the white light was just so intense, and he was intensely happy, and I'm no longer afraid to die. I know that when I die I'm going to a much better place."

Mom's account seems to indicate that Chris was aware that Mom had negative feelings toward him. His appearing to her, I believe, was to heal the hurt that he had caused by not wanting her to visit him while he was paralyzed. I believe that Chris appeared to Michele the first time because she needed to know that he was okay and happy in his new life. The second time, I believe he knew that at that moment she was hurting and needed to hug him and to be hugged by him. By appearing to her he was able to tell her that he still loved her and was concerned about her. Later I would read many accounts that indicate our deceased loved ones are able to contact us. Sometimes they come to right a wrong or to relieve anxiety or simply to tell us that they love us.

The experiences that Michele and Mom had with Chris further confirmed for me that God, in His concern for us, allows our loved ones to make themselves known to us in order to bring us peace and to reassure us that they will be with us when we need them. After her experience, Mom never doubted that Chris loved her. It brought her peace and serenity. She no longer felt deprived or angry because she had been unable to see him before he died. The night after Chris died Michele too experienced a healing of the spirit because she knew that Chris was happy.

Michele and Mom were overwhelmed by the intensity of the brilliant, white light. There is a parallel in the accounts of near-death experiences where the intensity of the light is often mentioned. However, neither Michele nor Mom had read any NDE accounts, nor did either of them know of the other's experience with Chris and the brilliant white light until weeks after they had occurred. They simply described their own experience.

Jack and I believe we saw Chris walking into the fraternity house at Purdue. We were passing through Lafayette, and decided to drive by the monument that Mark and the fraternity had erected on the grounds of the fraternity house. As we sat reminiscing and looking ahead at the frat house, several students walked along the sidewalk and entered the house. Jack and I spotted one young man at the same time - the same height, coloring, profile, and especially the way he carried his body and his walk. Chris had been paralyzed for almost eight months, had walked with difficulty for several months before that, and had been deceased for over a year. I had forgotten how he walked. This young man had Chris's exact stride. If Chris would have materialized anywhere, it surely would have been at his beloved Phi Kappa Psi frat house; he was showing us that he was totally happy now.

Doug, our son-in-law, who has very developed intuitive ability, has seen Chris three times. The first time Doug visited our home he slept in John's old room. In the early morning as Doug was waking up, he saw a young man standing in the doorway leaning one shoulder against the door frame with his arms casually folded across his chest. Doug was awake so he knew it wasn't a dream. Although he had never met Chris, he thought it could be Chris. When he came downstairs, he casually asked John if Chris used to come and talk to him in his room. John said yes, he would be lying in bed and Chris would come and stand in the doorway, lean against the door frame and chat.

The second time Doug saw Chris we were at Maryann and David's home celebrating Christmas. All of us were congregated in the living room opening gifts and snacking when Doug looked up and saw Chris looking in through the glass in the door. He was smiling and simply looking at all of us. And then he disappeared.

The third time, we were having dinner at the club where John and Chris used to play golf. The table at which we were sitting overlooked the creek that ran through several holes along the course. This time, as Doug looked at the creek below us he saw Chris as a young boy. Chris was crouched beside the creek holding a stick that he was poking into the water. Then the image was gone. He asked John if he and Chris had ever walked along the creek, to which John responded by recounting their many adventures hunting for golf balls. Doug finally shared his experiences with John, and after a few years he was able to share them with me. He had been reluctant to do so earlier because he had not wanted to intrude on our own personal experiences with Chris.

Recently, I had a reunion with three of my high school friends. Of the four, three of us have a special bond in that each of us has lost a child to cancer. In the course of our visit we talked about our deceased children, their ages, and type of cancer. Wishing to bring a note of hope, and hoping they would have experiences they would be willing to share, I related a few of the experiences we have had with Christopher. Regrettably, they had not had any experiences with their deceased children. I saw the disappointment on their faces as they shook their heads; and I regretted having shared my own before asking if they had had any unusual experiences. But things happen for a reason and I have to accept that. As I finished speaking, one friend said, "Therese, maybe you've had these experiences because you're open to having them."

Perhaps that's true because I did believe that Chris and I would always be connected in some way. But I'm not sure that my family believed as I did and yet they also have had experiences. Jack, Michele, Maryann, Jack's Mother, and Doug have had experiences with Chris and a total of fifteen of our friends have been with us at one time or another when Chris has made his presence known.

My friend who had not lost a child said, "There has to be a reason why your son is allowed to make his presence known and the others are not." She was insistent that, "These things are allowed to happen only for a reason."

I explained that the only reason I could think of was that I was writing a book about Chris's illness and death and the impact he has had on our lives. My friends thought that could be the reason why Chris was able to make himself known.

Since that luncheon I've reflected on the reason why Chris is able to "show up." Perhaps he wants to add his "voice" to those of other spirits who wish to bring to a troubled, doubting world, hope and awareness of the eternal life of the spirit.

I have come to believe that a soul exists before it takes on human form. There, in that pre-earth existence, each is presented with opportunities for the continued growth of the soul. One such opportunity involves becoming human. The purpose in coming to earth school is to grow spiritually, while at the same time agreeing to help others as they work through what Carolyn Myss calls "sacred tasks." Myss believes that, before coming to earth, groups of souls agree to learn and to help one another as they each fulfill their own sacred contract. It is my belief that some souls come simply as teachers of others as with those who are born severely retarded. They have no need to learn, they are here simply as teachers.

I believe that accepting God's will for Chris and caring for him was a sacred task, a major part of our sacred contract (agreement), that Chris and our family had made together in our pre-earth life, because his illness and death have had a profound effect on each of us and changed us.

Perhaps part of my sacred contract, indeed part of my family's sacred contract is to work with Christopher to bring comfort to those who grieve the loss of a loved one, and to bring hope to those who, doubting the immortality of the soul, only believe in a material world that ends when we die.

❧ 11 ☙

REFLECTION – MEDITATION – CHANGE

From early childhood I've believed in the life of the spirit and in the immortality of the soul. For this I thank my mother who told me in simple terms about God and heaven, and taught me my prayers. I'm also blessed to have had maternal and paternal grandmothers who lived their Christian beliefs simply and authentically. Parochial school religion classes and college philosophy and theology courses reinforced and more clearly defined my earlier concepts. But when I had doubts or questions I suppressed them; because before Vatican Council II, Catholics accepted without question all matters of faith and morals. When Pope John XX111 "opened the window" to let in fresh thought, I gave myself permission to question, to change, and to grow; and at that junction, to evaluate and synthesize theological concepts in the light of my own life and inner experiences.

But until Chris's illness one constant never changed - my great fear of God the Father, the just and vengeful God of the Old Testament. As a preschooler I had a holy card depicting an angel watching over a little boy and girl as they crossed a rickety wooden bridge, from which I concluded that angels protect us from harm. But rather than feeling happy and safe, the picture made me sad because I didn't want to be the little girl. I wanted to be the angel who was free to be with God instead of restricted to an earthly life. It wasn't until I entered first grade and was taught sin and punishment that I learned to fear God.

I learned that if I violated a commandment or law of the church, I would face punishment in purgatory or even hell. I was taught to perceive Him as the just judge and score keeper and the one who seemed to turn a deaf ear to my prayers. It was an anthropomorphic projection of God based on human failures, judgment and punishment – error being sinful, rather than an integral part of the human experience.

When fear colors our perceptions and motivates our actions it becomes a barrier to understanding and love. A tyrant is obeyed but is he loved? In my narrow view of God, I thought of him as the supremely harsh and severe ruler who had ultimate power over my body and mind and more importantly, over my immortal soul.

After the empty chair experience with God I understood that as a sensitive, impressionable, and fearful child I had internalized and accepted frightening concepts of God that were taught by religion teachers who focused on sin and the justice of God as they taught vulnerable and innocent children.

As an adult, after Vatican II, I tried to make sense of our humanness in the light of what I thought God expected of us. God created us as we are with all our failings and shortcomings. He made us miraculously and incredibly human with "feet of clay" and prone to making mistakes. Yet I had learned that He expected us to live as though we were perfect and would "become angry" if we did not live as if we were. If we died in the "state of mortal sin," that would be "it" for us. No second chance was preached as available! This seemed like a double bind and extremely unfair of God. Would God create us as vulnerable human beings and only give us one chance, one life to get it right?

My experience as a mother, especially caring for Chris during his devastating illness, changed my concept of God's love for us. Through my personal experiences I grasped how much God loves us, his children. If I, a simple human being, could care for Chris day in day out, putting his need for support, companionship, and love before my anguish and horror at watching helplessly as he grew steadily weaker and incapacitated, through an illness that would take his life; then how much more does God, the Source of Love care, love, understand, and support us, his children? If I, like mothers from time immemorial, did not abandon my child when life became harsh and painful, would God ever abandon us? If I could love my children unconditionally no matter what they did or what the cost, wouldn't God love us at least that much? If love means wanting with all my heart and soul love, joy, peace, and all good things for my children, could God, the Source of Love, deprive his children of life without Him and mete out the worst possible punishment - eternal banishment in a place of pain and suffering?

The empty chair experience revealed a generous God whose love is evident in our lives, in the beauty of our planet, and in the magnificence of the universe. When I walk along a sandy windswept beach, or gaze at the stars or experience a brilliant sunset, I know that God loves me. These are not the works of the tyrannical, impersonal God I was raised with, but rather a truer image of the most incredible lover that we will ever know.

I had a powerful experience several years ago when I listened to a dialogue between Joseph Campbell and Bill Moyers during which Campbell, while making a point, explained the distinction between heaven and eternity. He said that for us, heaven has a beginning and then it is everlasting, while eternity has no beginning and no end. If that is the case, Campbell went on, then we are living in eternity right now. Something so simple and logical had never occurred to me before. It was a shocking revelation, a peak moment that had a profound effect on me, because it offered a new and clarifying insight concerning human life.

I had been taught and believed that when I died and if I went to heaven, I would be with God for all eternity. I prayed I would be that blessed – life with God for all eternity! But now I learned that we are in eternity right now – which means that God is with us NOW – HERE and NOW. It is the good news that illuminates and changes my concept of God and life. Could this be what Jesus meant when he said, "The kingdom of God is here?" This moment, this time on earth is all a part of the kingdom, of eternity; and I don't have to wait for heaven to be with God because He is not at the end of the Universe. He is at the center of everything, at the center of my being. I am not God, but each breath I take is the breath of life that comes from the Creator. I am not apart from God – I am surrounded by Him. I swim in an ocean of God. "O heavenly King, Comforter, Spirit of Truth, You are everywhere present, and fill all things." This beautiful prayer is an excerpt from the *Prayer Service in Honor of Christ the Lover of Mankind* in the Eastern Rite Catholic Church. Without stating the obvious, namely that we are in eternity now, it supports the concept.

While in graduate school I learned the following mantra, similar to St. Patrick's Breastplate prayer: "God is above me, God is beneath me. God is in front of me. God is behind me. God is on my right side. God is on my left side. Wherever I am, God is - and all is well." This too, is a comforting prayer that serves to remind me that I am always surrounded by the loving God who gives me protection, love, and support.

All life is connected because we are all joined to the Divine Source of all life, the Creator; therefore we are all one in Him. And so our prayer is, "I unite myself to all life from the beginning of time and I acknowledge You as Source." Our prayers are inclusive rather than exclusive. When praying for a friend or a loved one with a problem - we also ask for divine help for everyone having the same problem. When we believe that we are one with God, the Source of All, then we live out that belief in all of our actions including our prayers; otherwise, there is discord between what we believe and how we live.

After Chris died, I read about the lives of the mystics, and it broadened my concept of spiritual reality and possibility. I finally comprehended that they served God out of great love for him, not because they feared him. I had not internalized this concept until recently. Francis of Assisi, Catherine of Siena, Mechtild of Magdeburg, Terese of Avila were transformed by their love of God.

In his biography of St. Therese of Lisieux, *Light Of The Night,*

Jean-Francois Six quotes St. Therese, "He knows our frailty. He remembers we are only dust. As a father has tenderness for his children, so the Lord has compassion on us.... my way is all confidence and love. I do not understand souls who fear a Friend so tender."

If as children we were given a truer concept of the loving God (rather than having fear of God instilled in our impressionable hearts) then early on we would respond to life's challenges out of love, serve God and each other out of love, live fully the best way we could out of love, not from fear of eternal damnation. Then the world would be a different place.

In the ensuing years I have read other books that reinforce my new awareness of the Father's love, among them: *Original Blessing*, Matthew Fox, *Care Of The Soul*, Thomas Moore, *The Seat Of The Soul*, Gary Zukov, *Teresa of Avila*, translated by Kavanaugh and Rodriguez, and *Thirsting For God*, Mother Teresa.

I discovered the works of Anthony deMello, S.J., particularly his book *Awareness*. His was a fresh voice that gave me an image of a larger God that encouraged and validated my reality and emerging beliefs. The fact that he was a Jesuit gave me the courage to read, question, and change my narrow belief about God and my relationship to him. I first learned of deMello from a friend who gave me a series of retreat questions. His first question shocked me and blew apart the belief that even though Jesus has forgiven our sins, a good Christian should remember past transgressions with great remorse. Whereas deMello asks, "Why do you spend even a moment worrying about something you did in the past? Wake up!"

These authors have helped me to come to a sounder understanding of God's expectations of us. I have given myself permission to take God out of the narrow box in which he resided for years.

As a preschooler I heard my Italian grandmother refer to peccato – sin. I thought it meant mistake. Perhaps I wasn't wrong – isn't sin a mistake, an error in judgment? Our priest friend puts it beautifully. He said, "When a toddler is learning to walk it falls, gets up, falls again, gets up again and then finally, one day, it walks. And we call that growth. Why were we taught that falling was a sin?" Isn't sin a failing, a falling, a mistake? And maybe we fall many times before we finally get it right and can walk. Does God who created us, judge us for the times we fall; or does He watch with love and compassion because, having created us, He knows who we are – fragile beings simply trying to make our way in this life as we struggle toward growth?

I can no longer conceive that this God of Love could banish a child of his creation forever. I can no longer look at a newborn child and believe that if it were not baptized it would not be with God. Baptism is the outward sign that recognizes and celebrates the truth – that we are Children of God. Only a very illogical theologian could invent a contradictory theory that a loving God and parent would let anyone of his children live for all eternity in a place where He is not present.

Is there a place where God is not present? Hell is the absence of light and love, a state of pain and loss. Most of us have been to hell a few times in our lives – others in war torn countries have lived their entire lives in fear and trembling. That truly is hell, and it exists during our human life. Would the loving Father, of whom Jesus speaks, allow his own children to suffer for all eternity?

Jesus said, "In my Father's House there are many mansions." Perhaps the statement refers to the possibility that there are many stages of growth throughout the eternal life of the soul. As we grow, God moves us to the level that will best serve the continued growth of our soul.

There are many stages in the growth of the soul, and earth school is only one of them. My belief seems to be validated by the accounts of those who have had NDEs. I learned from these accounts of near death experiences that upon meeting the being of light, the soul experiences a review of its life which is meant to "provoke reflection." In many cases, the soul felt such terrible remorse that it did not think it could stand another instant of the review, but in none of these accounts was the soul condemned. During the review, the NDEers felt warmth and love coming from the being of light, not condemnation. They believed the review was given so that they could learn from it, because learning continues into the next life.

To quote one account from Moody's, *Life After Life,* the being of light

"was there with me the whole time, he carried me back through the flashback because I felt his presence, and because he made comments here and there. He was trying to show me something in each one of these flashbacks. It's not like he was trying to see what I had done- he knew already-but he was picking out these certain flashbacks of my life and putting them in front of me so that I would have to recall them. All through this, he kept stressing the importance of love.....He pointed out to me that I should do things for other people, and to do my best. There was-n't any accusation in any of this, though. When he came across times when I had been selfish, his attitude was only that I had been learning from them, too."

When these NDEers returned from their experience, they were profoundly changed - in the way they lived, in what was important to them, in how they treated others. They were not doing it because they were afraid of the consequences, but out of love and a change in their understanding of what matters in this life.

I recently saw a television special on Pope John Paul II in which the Pope stated that we must express whatever feeling we have toward God – be it anger, rage, or doubt. We must not stop. We must go into the feeling because at that point we are very close to faith. That is what happened to me when I put God in the empty chair. I had reached the point where I was so broken and desperate, in so much anguish that I was forced to confront God with my rage, anger, rejection and pain. It was then that fear fell away and love entered, and I was able to trust in God and to see with new eyes. At that moment, my personal relationship with Him began.

I know now, that God loves me and cherishes me just as I am – imperfect, prone to anger, "warts and all"– total acceptance in the here and now of eternity! He knows I love him and He is with me now, not waiting until I make the transition. Further, He has never banished nor abandoned me - rather He has given me angels and guides to help me through this passage called life. Perhaps my higher self, my soul, the part of me that has always been connected to the Father has always known this; but my conscious self was not aware. Loving and caring for Christopher through his illness and death brought me from fear of the Father to blinding rage because He had inflicted cancer on my son, and finally to awareness of His total and all abiding love for me.

This awareness has changed the focus of my life. This new relationship with God, that is based on love not on fear as it once was, has made the biggest difference in my life and one for which I am most grateful. Now I think of God as the Loving Creator ever creating new possibilities in our lives. He is Lord of the Dance and the Dancer and we are being danced. He is Perfection, Stillpoint, and we are the movement around Him as we move toward growth. He is First Cause and Uncaused Cause, The Alpha and The Omega. He is Abba, Yahweh, Mother, the loving Father about whom Jesus spoke - the gentle, forgiving, nurturing Father who loves and understands us as we have always yearned to be loved and understood. He is the generous Lover who lays the beauty of the universe at our feet. He is the Counselor who sends His angels in all their forms to teach and guide us. He is the Comforter and faithful friend who is there through trial and tribulation. He is the God of Unknowing shrouded in mystery. He is our heart's desire.

Life did not change and become easier after Chris died. But

what has changed is the way I perceive problems. Before, when difficult situations arose, I would become angry, resentful, and even paranoid, asking, "why me?" I'd struggle through one difficulty after another feeling all of those emotions. I thought road blocks were sent by God to punish me. I translated that to mean He didn't love me.

Now I understand that difficulties are a part of the human condition through which I can learn something that my soul needs to work through, and through which I'm invited to grow and to change. It is only an invitation because I have the freedom of will to accept or reject it. But if I have a desire to grow spiritually, it's up to me to accept the opportunities and problems that present themselves, no matter how difficult, and allow them to change me. Now when challenging situations arise, I try to remember to ask myself what I'm being called to learn. It is not always clear or easy, but ultimately I know it's about spiritual growth.

Life did not get easier - what changed was my perception. It seems to me that once one says yes to God, meaning yes to growing aspects of one's soul, the opportunities for growth seem to come more rapidly. Seven years ago, our son, John, during his last few months of internship in Denver, called to say he would be home for the weekend. He had something important to tell us. It was good to have him home even for a short time as we had not seen him for several months and we missed him. After finishing dinner on Saturday evening, he asked Jack and me to sit down so he could talk to us.

He looked anxious as he said, "Mom and Dad, I have something to tell you. I have known for quite a while that I'm gay, and I'm telling you because I want you to know who I am, and that I am no longer going to keep this part of me hidden."

As I really looked at him, I saw his soul in his eyes and I heard so much that he wasn't saying – "Please accept me, please love me anyway, please don't reject me."

Tears came to my eyes as I said, "Oh! John, you've picked

such a hard life."

He replied, "No, Mom, it's picked me!"

I knew that to be the truth, because although he was in his late thirties and not married, I knew he had many women friends. I had met many of the beautiful, intelligent, successful women that he had dated, and I felt that once he finished his professional training which had come later in his life, he would find the right woman to marry. Chris's illness and death had taken its toll on him, and was instrumental in his leaving a successful career to pursue a new course. I felt it was only a matter of time before he met the right woman.

As we continued to listen to him, he explained that he had really tried, but he was unable to sustain relationships with women even though he wanted to. No one wants to be different, especially when it carries an enormous social stigma. But at a point in his life and professional training he had had to address the denial of his authentic self. If he was to work with clients encouraging them to be authentic, he realized he had to face, accept, and embrace his own reality.

Jack and I told him that we loved him and with our blessing, he left for Denver. Now reality set in. We would never have a daughter-in-law and experience the joy of loving his children. I was afraid for him. Would he have to face personal and professional rejection and ostracism? Should we tell our family and friends? How would they react? Did they have stereotypic views of gays? I have several gay friends and acquaintances that I respect and admire. They are spiritual, intelligent, hardworking, loving people who are making contributions in the fields of business, education, and the arts. But I was not totally without bias. I just never thought I would have to deal with this issue too.

On Monday morning I drove to Mass feeling very sad, with a great burden on my shoulders. I thought of the anguish we had all endured during Chris's illness, now God had placed another difficulty before us. This time we were being called to deal with all the issues around having a son who is gay.

As I sat in church I gradually became aware that I was feeling very sorry for myself. It was all about what I wanted to have and what I would not have –a son with a life style that was acceptable by the church and society, a daughter-in-law, grand-children. It was all about my losses and fears of what the church and society thought of gays; how they would judge him and as a result, us. I knew that most parents were embarrassed by their gay children because of the social stigma and religious prejudice. I could understand their fear. I had been a people-pleaser most of my life. As a first generation American I had always simply wanted to conform. To be different was to invite attention and criticism.

I asked myself if I could ever reject one of my children, and the answer that immediately sprang from my heart was, never. Could God ever ask me to reject my son? From the depths of my soul I knew that I would not turn away nor would God. To reject him would be to go against my soul and everything that I had learned since Chris's death. To conform to social or religious pressure at this point in my life would feel like a straight jacket. I had grown beyond believing that the loving God would condemn any child of His creation. I did not want to put Him back into the narrow box from which I had released Him. If I believed that God would not banish or abandon me, could I believe that He would banish my son or anyone for being gay? God had opened me to a desire to be more loving not to withhold it. I had to let go of Chris, but I knew in my heart that God was not asking me to let go of John, rather He was calling me once again to grow. I had learned to be inclu-sive, not exclusive; and now I was being called to deal with my own fear and residual prejudice, and to live what I believed.

During Mass it occurred to me that all I was being called to do was to love. That is all. John had not changed; he was the same perceptive, intelligent, amusing and caring son that I had always known and loved. He was the one who had come home every weekend for the better part of a year so that he could be with his dying brother. All I was called to do was to continue to love him, and that had never been a hardship – it had always been a joy. I understood that God, who created him and loved him, had given John the perfect life situation that he needed to grow fully. At the same time, through him, we too were being called to stretch and grow. I thought about what I was being called to learn from this, and the answer was that I had to have the courage to rise above my own fears and desire for conformity and live authentically.

Gradually the way became clear and simple –I would accept this new turn that our lives had taken, including whatever criticism the church and society would make. I would accept the loss of grandchildren and a daughter-in-law, understanding that it was not meant for John to have a wife or children. It was not part of his journey, and so not part of ours either. God had given him and so us, a different path.

By the end of Mass, I knew I wanted to openly accept him. I would not hide his identity from family and friends. He deserved our open and honest support for who he was. When I told Jack that I wanted to give John our full support and love, he agreed with all his heart. In the next week we spoke with family and friends and told them that John was gay. To their credit and to John's, they fully accepted him. What a miracle of support and affection!

Three months later we proudly watched as he received his Doctor of Psychology degree and the Distinguished Graduate Award. Later, at a celebration dinner, we met his partner, Doug, who like John was raised Catholic, attended parochial school, and has a strong sense of morality and love of family. Both are perceptive, intelligent, and loving human beings. Like John he is loved by our children and grandchildren. We are a happier family because they are a vital part of it.

None of my fears became reality. They are welcomed by our extended family and friends. John has a professional position with a firm that knows he is gay and appreciates his professional ability. Instead of a daughter-in-law, we have another fine son-in-law. And now we have Aidan, our bi-racial granddaughter whom John and Doug adopted knowing they will face many challenges as a gay couple with bi-racial children. They are warm, responsible, loving parents and Aidan is a sweet, contented infant. They understand that the situations they will encounter will be opportunities for their growth. Seven years later, I know that God gave me the grace to make an enlightened decision and our lives are richer for it.

The most profound change in my life is that I don't blame God when I am faced with problems. I have learned to accept tragedies and problems without anger or rage toward God even when we have lost other members of our family. My father, both of my sisters, and several other family members have made the transition to the next life and have joined Chris. But the insights that I have had since Chris died have helped me to accept their deaths, because I learned that when one's life work is completed, the soul moves on. I'm comforted by the belief that we do not lose those whom we have loved. They participate in our lives by guiding and praying for us and sometimes, as with Chris, by making their presence known.

Since Chris's illness I have had a great desire to learn whatever I can about life after death. I had several motives. First, I was searching for validation of the awesome and humbling experiences that continue to this day, and affirm that Chris is able to reach us, his earthly family. Second, I wanted to understand what Chris was experiencing on the other side and what all of us will some day experience. And lastly, I wanted to have a better understanding not only of the meaning of death but also of the meaning of life.

My desire and my experiences motivated me to search for concrete answers, and I found them in the direct near death experiences of persons who had returned to report them. I read many books on the subject, among them, Betty Eadie's own experience in *Embraced By The Light*, plus authors, Kubler

Ross and Raymond Moody, both of whom describe in great detail their patients' fascinating experiences and how their attitudes toward their present lives changed and transformed them. I reasoned that what NDEers experienced was the same as those of people who died and did not return - at least initially their experiences were the same. I reasoned that if that were possible for someone having a near death experience, then that and so much more would be possible for Chris.

I read accounts written by gifted mediums like Rosemary Altea, Edgar Cayce, and James Van Praagh who assisted people in contacting their deceased love ones. These accounts further affirm that our loved ones continue to care for us, wish to relieve any anxieties we may have concerning them, and want us to know that they are happy. Some are able to communicate with us in a manner that leaves no doubt as to whom they are.

From our own experiences and receiving validation from these books, I came to believe that when I spoke to Chris, he would hear me. There were times, especially during the first couple of years, when I felt his energy swirling around me, and I became lightheaded because his presence was so real.

I had been content with my life until Chris's illness and death shook me to the core and led me to a new place, where I received glimpses of spiritual vistas that opened in me a great desire to deepen my spiritual awareness and live a more spiritually centered life. This desire led me on a quest for more knowledge; and I read angel stories, the books of Donald Nicholl, Brian Weiss, books on the Tao, writings of the mystics, books by theologians. I attended workshops and participated in discussion groups.

I met several gifted women, one of whom I am privileged to call my friend - conscious medium, Angel Gail. Another is a Dominican nun who has the ability to read auras. Both of these women have been of great help to me in my spiritual development.

Through affiliation with The Association for Humanistic Psychology, I attended a conference presented by the Institute of

Noetic Science, an organization that is on the cutting edge of learning and spiritual exploration. The conference, entitled *Life, Death, and the Survival of Consciousness* included distinguished presenters from many disciplines: psychologists, researchers, scientists, writers, anthropologists, a world-renowned healer, an astronaut, and an author who had had a NDE. I did not attend as a skeptic who needed convincing that there is life after death; because my faith, our family experiences, and the books I was reading had convinced me that death is merely a transition to the next life. Rather, it was to hear what scholars from many disciplines believed.

The conference was very well attended, indicating that many others are on a search for knowledge about ultimate truths. It was an enriching and exciting conference from which I learned many things. One of the conclusions that I drew after listening to many of the gifted presenters, was that they all believed that life does not end when the body dies. Something survives. Some presenters, the scientists, called it consciousness, some presenters called it the soul, and others called it the spirit.

Readings, reflections, conferences, and our family experiences have led me to a new understanding of our purpose for taking human form. It seems to me that we come to learn and to grow dimensions of our souls, so that ultimately we grow in our ability to love. As fragile, limited human beings we can only surmise because who but God, the author of life can comprehend its mystery? Perhaps we will have a better understanding in the next life. But based on reflection, meditation, and readings, I believe that the soul exists before it is joined to the body at the moment of conception and begins life in human form. In that pre-earth life, the soul wishing to grow and without knowing the particular circumstances into which it will be born, cooperates with God and says "send me!"

Each of us has a life plan. Everything that happens to us in our lifetime has purpose. Situations that arise are meant to assist and teach us and others, and help us to grow in love and understanding. The circumstances into which we are born are perfect for each soul's growth. The individuals who constitute our family and friends have special meaning; they are not an accident of birth. At a soul level we agree to help each other as we continue in our journey toward growth. As we grow dimensions of our soul, we are at the same time instrumental in helping others to grow. I saw this so visibly in Chris's life and in my sister, Joanne's life as she lived with diabetes for thirty-five heroic years.

Specific events and life situations such as cancer, poverty, diabetes, and other devastating and challenging circumstances with which we are faced are ones that will best serve us, so that through them we have the opportunity to learn and to grow in love. What matters is how we perceive, react to, and grow as a result of them. I believe this is the reason we take on human form. We may often feel that we are struggling through these earthly challenges alone, but we are not. We have been given guardian angels and guides to assist us in working through different phases of our life plan.

From time immemorial man has asked if there is a purpose to human suffering and pain. It seems incomprehensible that anything good can come from it. Why must we endure pain or watch helplessly as some one we love suffers? Budda said, "To be in human form is to suffer." Whether we understand it or not, suffering and pain are a reality of our human condition. Perhaps the reason that we must endure them is because they are conducive to the development and increase of heroic human and spiritual virtues and values. Perhaps our souls grow in wisdom, patience, perseverance, courage and other gifts of the spirit as the result of our being tested. Through trial and tribulation are we human beings invited to develop the higher potentialities of our personality, character, and spirit? I believe that we are.

There was no miracle of healing for Christopher in spite of the daily prayers said for him by all of us and by so many caring people during the eighteen months of his illness, months that tested the outer limits of his physical and emotional endurance. He lost freedom and independence when he lost the ability to walk and to drive. In the months that followed, he continued to lose freedom and control over his life. He could not stand under a shower to bathe himself and to shampoo his hair. He was unable to turn in bed without two people and a draw-sheet to assist him. He lost bowel and bladder control, with the resultant embarrassment of needing assistance. He had to cope with excruciating pain and depended on morphine to get him through. He endured the almost daily complications, frequent bladder infections, and the ever-present low-grade fevers that kept him hot and uncomfortable. He put up with increased pain and difficulty eating. And in addition to all that, he had to deal with the knowledge that even this limited existence would end. For Chris the most difficult aspect of all was having to give up his studies and all his dreams for the future. There was no future, only the painful present and that would soon come to an end.

We watched helplessly as the illness ravaged his body and appearance. Chris's once handsome face became long, gray, and thin, his thick black hair turned thin and lifeless, and his beautiful expressive eyes grew sad and tired. His upper body became thin and emaciated, while his enlarged liver and poor circulation caused his lower body to become edematous and misshapen.

Despite the most advanced medical treatments none were of help to Christopher. Surgery had not stopped the spread of cancer. He was rejected for the Interteukin II protocol. Embolization might have worked – but did not. There was no miracle. The prayers did not open the door to miracle drugs or procedures. There was no unaccounted for healing. We watched in agony as our beloved son suffered, became disfigured and emaciated, and then died.

We can't fathom the mysterious "mind' of God, the Cloud of Unknowing. We don't know how the universe works. We don't know or understand why some recover from catastrophic illness while others, like Chris, do not recover. It seems in those instances of recovery that the natural law is suspended because they seem to recover when everything is against recovery. Against all odds! It is a miracle!

But, like Chris, most do not receive a miracle of healing, no matter how many prayers are said for their recovery. Despite great medical efforts to keep them alive, they die. At those times it seems as though God is not listening, and worse, does not love us or care that someone we love is suffering. That is exactly what I believed at the onset of Chris's illness. We couldn't understand why Chris had to endure cancer at his young age, and why he had to die from it. Why did we as a family have to have our hearts broken? I was convinced that God was not listening to our fervent prayers or simply did not care. I no longer believe that is the reason that most people do not recover.

I believe the answer is in the soul's plan for its own growth. Perhaps, although on the human level the person wishes to recover, the soul does not wish to go on living. It is ready to move on. The spirit knows it has finished its work here, and understands that God has other plans for its continued growth. And so it moves on. If we understand this, then death is not failure on the part of family and medicine to keep a loved one alive. And more importantly it is not punishment from an uncaring, unloving God. From a human perspective it may seem so, but not from the spiritual perspective because life does not end when we die. Life as we know it in this human body is only one step in the life and growth of our souls. Long life on the human plane is not necessarily a reward. Perhaps it simply takes longer for some souls to complete their growth here.

On a human level Chris wanted to live to fulfill all of his dreams. But his soul had other plans for his future. I have wondered if Chris and others who die young, asked on a soul level for a life situation that would move them rapidly through their life's work and purpose. It seems to me that is what happened with Christopher. His soul grew as he endured the trials and tribulations of his disease. Though he was physically trapped in his hospital bed in the family room his soul soared and climbed mountains.

There was no miracle of healing for Chris. But I believe there was another kind of miracle, one of transformation. Because, as Chris lost physical abilities, other, non-physical qualities developed. He grew in gifts of the spirit: remarkable courage and endurance, patience, detachment from material things, faith and trust in God, maturity, wisdom, and love. While cancer was disfiguring and destroying his body, his spirit was growing stronger.

During the months that I spent with him I witnessed his spiritual growth. He faced cancer surgery, excruciatingly painful invasive procedures, and paralysis with undaunted courage and perseverance. As he became more incapacitated he had to relinquish more freedom and control, and he quietly accepted it. The week in October, when he became paralyzed, was the only time when his anger made life unbearable. But even then he didn't cry out, "Why me?" Or "Why is God doing this to me?" The rest of the family asked those questions but Chris didn't. He was heartbroken that he would not have the future that he dreamed of, but he did not blame God or lash out at him. In fact during our quiet prayer time together at night, he expressed fear that he had not done enough with his life to merit heaven. God didn't owe him. He owed God. It was faith and trust in God's plan for him that helped him to accept the turn his life had taken.

Chris loved his possessions, especially his Honda CRX, his computer, and the train set he and John had collected and worked on since early childhood. As difficult as it must have been for him to accept more losses, he came to the realization that he would no longer need material things, and he detached himself from the possessions that he loved. He could have chosen to leave the burden and the pain of disposing of them to us after he was gone, but he didn't. Courageously he took responsibility for giving them to those he loved. After quiet reflection, he thoughtfully gave them and his savings to his brother and sisters. He did it quietly and without fanfare. He spoke with each individually when they came to visit him, and gave them a gift that was not merely material but one from his heart. We watched him gradually let go of everything material and physical as he moved into the world of the spirit. It did not happen at the moment of his death. It had been happening slowly and gradually through the last several months, until, on May 5th he no longer needed his body and he became pure spirit.

❀ 12 ❀

FROM THE HEART –
JACK, MARYANN, MICHELE, JOHN

W hen Terese Fabbri spoke at the prayer service for Chris she called him: teacher. She said, "He accomplished every teacher's dream - to so touch their students' lives that they would change and grow. Chris was a teacher of the highest caliber because he touched so many lives with his person that each one grew, changed and became better because their path has crossed his and they would never be the same."

Christopher did change us and we would never be the same. Having witnessed his courage, endurance, and faith, in the face of great physical and emotional suffering and death, we never could wish to return to our old selves. And the miracle we had been praying and searching for became the transformation of our lives. Each of us was impacted by Chris. In the following accounts Jack, Maryann, Michele, and John share memories and insights as they relate to their life journey with Chris.

Jack went through the whole experience with Chris and me, and much of what I have written applies to him too. He didn't want to duplicate what I have already said. But he did want to share some of his own reflections.

"I have so many memories of Christopher. I have to smile when I remember a family trip to Mt. Vernon when we lost five year old Chris. We found him sitting on a bench waiting for us to return to the nearby parking lot. He said he wasn't lost. He knew where he was. He had fol-lowed the crowd back to the parking area and was waiting for us knowing that we would eventually be returning to the car.

I have a wonderful memory of a golf trip to Pinehurst that I took with Chris and John. One afternoon after play-

ing golf Chris tried to keep up with John and ate a huge
hot fudge sundae and fries at Hojo's and then could not eat
supper. We ate in a Cracker Barrel restaurant for the first
time on that trip and the boys couldn't get enough of the
biscuits and fruit cobblers.

I remember winning the father and son golf tournament
with each of the boys and then John, Chris and I won the
club's first ethnic open. They loved winning the trophy
and they loved splitting the prizes even more.

I can never forget the sad trip to the National Institute of
Health in Washington over Labor Day 1986 and all the sad
trips to doctors and hospitals during Chris's illness.

I remember how it changed me.

Christopher's illness struck me like a truck going ninety
miles an hour. It was totally unexpected. When we were at
the University Hospital in Chicago in February of 1986 waiting for the test results, I remember going over to his chart
and reading the X-ray report at the nurse's station. I almost
wished that I had not done that. Now I knew what Dr.
Peters was going to tell us when he came to give us the test
results. I really did not want to hear it. I hoped that the pre-
liminary report was wrong. It wasn't!

This now started a process in my life that was new to me.
My total being was now focused on someone outside of
myself. I was going to devote my entire energy to try to
save Chris from dying. I gave up all outside activities to be
with him as much as I could. We took him to Florida to
Long Boat Key. He loved it. But even down there I was
apprehensive about his nagging backache. I feared the
original tumor had spread.

A week later, when we returned I found out that this was
so. I now knew that Chris was going to die. I was furious
with God, and I could not understand why He would take
this wonderful spirit so soon and leave me here. I would
have switched places if I were given the choice.

Therese gave me some books to read and they did a lot to diminish the mental pain that I felt. I thought about him around the clock. I watched him go through terrifying tests that I knew were very painful and I wanted to lie down and do them for him.

Towards the end I was tempted to move the process along to shorten his suffering. I reasoned that no one would know except God and afterwards Chris would know. I could handle that. But I knew that he was not ready to let go yet and I knew it was wrong. My faith and the knowledge that Chris would not want me to do something sinful kept me from doing it.

The entire experience of being with Chris during his illness and death changed the way I worked with people. I grew in compassion and I gave more of myself to my patients' needs. If they took longer because they were hurting in places no one could see, I was more patient. I brought God into the office and I asked people to turn inward and seek God's help.

After Chris died I was asked by the Indiana State Medical Association to return to the Board of Directors and the conga line towards the presidency of the state medical society. I was flattered and honored. It was a plateau that I had worked toward for eighteen years, and now it was being offered to me with no strings or opposition. But I thought about how close our family had become during 1986 and 1987. If I accepted, it would mean traveling downstate and across the state several times a month. I would be sacrificing my family for MY GLORY. I did not want to go back to the old Jack. I think that was a lesson that the SPIRIT has taught me. I was really happy with the growth in all of our relationships with one another. There was so much to lose for so little. It was not even a tough choice. To this day I have not regretted it for one minute.

Having gone through this with Chris and our family, I

find that when I face a difficult situation, I compare it to what Chris went through, and what we all went through with him, and everything pales compared to Chris's ordeal. I don't think that I fear death as much now because it would reunite me with Chris. I feel strongly now about life after life. I believe that Chris is in heaven and having a ball.

He has answered my prayers many times, especially when I have needed help solving mechanical problems because he knows I have very little experience in that area. He has not failed to answer when I have asked him for help. I recall one day last fall when I felt overwhelmed by the task ahead of me. I had to move two truckloads of wet sand from the driveway to the area we were landscaping. We live in a beach community where most of the homes are occupied only during the summer and weekends. There was no one around to help me. I asked Chris to help me to find a solution to my problem. Within twenty minutes a truck loaded with a bulldozer rumbled down our street. He was on his way to do some work down the street but since the people were not at home there was no urgency. He said he would be happy to move the wet sand for me. That was help enough but ten minutes later another truck with another bulldozer came down our usually quiet street. I guess Chris wanted to make sure that I had plenty of help.

I believe that Chris's spirit came here to teach us to love, and that is exactly what he accomplished. Christ did the same thing and both suffered, died and left indelible marks on us all."

Maryann shared the following:
"I've thought often about the reason why as individuals and as a family we were given this suffering. Perhaps we needed to grow and change as individuals and as a family. I've seen a lot of changes in my brother, sister, parents and in myself because we went through the agony of Chris's

illness and death. For one thing it has strengthened all of
our relationships. It has taken me a long time to come to
the realization that as much as it was a painful experience, I
can see that our family journey with Chris brought about
life transforming changes. I still wish that we didn't have
to lose Chris to make the changes that we made.

Chris's illness and death changed my belief about medicine. I guess until then I felt that medicine could cure,
could help, could heal. I hadn't really come face to face
with medicine being unable to cure. Because medicine was
unable to cure Chris, I am now more afraid of sickness and
illness in my own children. On the positive side, because I
experienced Chris's illness and death, I feel that I am a
more sensitive physician. I'm more comfortable dealing
with someone who is dying. Because I am not afraid to
feel my feelings, I can be with the person as one human
being to another. Now I understand the pain and agony
that families go through when they are losing a loved one,
and so I feel that I am more empathic and compassionate.

One thing that I learned after losing Chris at such a young
age is to live in the present moment. Right now is important
because we only have today. We can't assume that we will
have time later to do what we want to do and to change how
we want to live. But it is a very difficult concept and belief
to live by. I try to remind myself of that when I feel down,
and when I start worrying about what is going to happen
tomorrow. I try to be mindful that when I worry about yesterday or tomorrow, I'm ruining today. So I try to enjoy
each day. I approach life from the viewpoint that I want to
spread a little cheer to someone every day. Each day I try to
perform an act of kindness and make someone smile each
day. I try to teach this to my children too.

I have some special memories of Chris when he was little. He used to manage to spill his glass of milk on my lap
just about every morning. It usually meant that I had to

change into a fresh uniform until I learned to react very quickly, jumping out of my seat before the milk made it to the edge of the table. I remember losing Chris at Mount Vernon. We were all terrified that he was lost, little peanut that he was.

Later when Chris was in high school and I came home to visit during medical school we would pal around together. He was a continuous source of knowledge. I asked him for his advice on so many things even though he was six years younger that I. He would drive me around in my car just so that I would not have to drive. I remember that he drove me to garage sales because I needed some things for my apartment. I have two dishes left from a set that I bought when he was with me. They are precious to me because, whenever I use them, I remember those times that we had together.

I have a poignant memory of the last time that I saw Chris alive. It was Sunday. He died on Tuesday morning. Before I left I kissed him and said goodbye to him. As I left the room I turned to look at him, and our eyes locked and held. At that moment we both knew that this was the last moment we would have together.

I believe that Chris is happy and in a better place now. I believe very strongly that life goes on after we die. I don't know how individuals who don't believe in life after death can deal with losing a loved one. My faith in life after death helped me to accept that Chris was going to die because I knew that some day I would see him again.

Now he is my connection to the spiritual world. He is a special person to talk to. Chris helps me not to be afraid to die. He is there for me. He'll come to get me when I die. I think Chris is my guardian angel now. I feel he made himself known to me on one occasion. I was sitting in a rocker nursing my son, Dominic in his room. The room was dark. Suddenly I thought I heard a cat crying or a baby crying. The sound was coming from an area high up near the ten foot ceiling. But there was no way a cat or a baby could be that high up. I immediately thought it must be Chris. The next day Mom told me of her experience at the same time of the evening. We both figured it was Chris telling us he was with us.

There are three distinct times when I think that Chris was protecting me. One was when I was skiing in a Birkebiner cross-country race. I was going down a very steep icy hill, and I started to stumble because someone in the track ahead of me had fallen. If I had gone down, I would have been badly hurt with a couple of broken bones. I remember coming through that and instantly thinking that Chris must have been with me, helping me.

I recall another time when I was going down a very steep icy driveway with all the kids in the car, and part of the wheel of our Suburban went over the edge. I was terrified that I would lose control of the van, and it would roll over the edge of the driveway, and on to the street below. It took an hour as I tried to carefully maneuver the van back onto the driveway. I remember thinking, when the kids and I were safe, that Chris must have been with us, guiding me.

The most recent time was last winter when I was driving on an expressway. I was driving fast and ended up in a ditch. I knew that Chris was working hard because despite the fact that there were semi-trucks next to me and behind me, I came out of it without a scratch.

I think of Chris often. I believe he wants me to be a good wife, mother, sister, daughter, friend, and last but not least a good physician. And that is what I wish for myself."

Michele wrote:
"My first remembrance of Chris was when my Mother was pregnant. I would look at her growing stomach with awe and wonderment, thinking that soon I would have a lit-

tle brother or sister. It was truly a miracle.

When Mom brought Chris home from the hospital I was so excited. Here was my new little brother with these huge eyes and tons of hair. He was so beautiful… but he was always crying. I remember trying to sleep but I couldn't because Chris was crying so loud and long. Something was wrong. He always cried. I'd lay in bed and pray that God would make Chris happy and well. I didn't want my little brother to be in pain. I wanted him to laugh. He deserved to be happy. We finally learned that he was allergic to fat. The fat in milk was causing him to have bloating and discomfort. This is what made him cry all the time. Finally, thank God he would be better. Not only was he better, he was a joy, a light in my life.

Growing up Chris and I shared a very special bond, despite our four year age difference. Maybe it was because I was the second daughter and he was the second son. I'm not sure why, but I felt a very strong connection to him. He had a marvelous wit and intellect. He was curious and enthusiastic about everything, from the trivial to the profound. He always explored new avenues, getting his hands, head, and heart into anything that came his way. His eyes would widen and one could see his brain churning. Chris was a brilliant, shining star with the potential to do anything he wanted with great success and skill. I was extremely proud to have him as my brother.

I never worried about Chris. No matter what came along, I knew that Chris could figure it out and take care of it. But there was one thing he couldn't take care of …..his cancer! When Mom and Dad told me Chris was home from college because he was having pain, I just assumed it was some minor problem that would be quickly diagnosed and cured. It wasn't to be. I remember exactly where and when I received the phone call from Mom and Dad telling me that Chris had cancer. It almost feels like yesterday. It was in the evening. I had come home from work and I was standing in the kitchen of my apartment. I felt as though I had been kicked in the stomach by a horse. Kicked so hard that the air was sucked out of me. It took a very long time for the reality of his illness to sink in. I couldn't internalize the reality. I couldn't believe Chris wouldn't be around; I wouldn't hear his voice or his laugh. I wouldn't see his smiling eyes. But it did sink in. It became reality when I went to see Chris at the hospital after his surgery. I looked in his eyes and I knew. His eyes, always bright, had lost hope. I saw it. I felt it deep in my soul.

I was angry, angry with God. How could he do this? It was horrifically unfair. Here was my beautiful, brilliant, loving little brother suffering, struggling, and dying. It was my fault! I wasn't a good person! I wasn't faithful enough! I wasn't.... It has taken me years to come to terms with Chris's illness and death. I'm no longer angry with God. I am truly, truly grateful. God gave us all, the most wonderful, magnificent gift. He blessed our lives no matter how short the time we had with him. He touched us deeply and profoundly and he changed our lives through his courage, love, and faith. He was my very special, very loving brother who will always be in my life whether or not he is living or dead. But there is still that large void that can never be replaced by his death, and I wish I could fill it.

Our family has become very close since Chris's death, closer than I ever dreamed possible. We express our love more. We are more tolerant of each other. We look out for one another.

The most important things I've learned from Chris and his illness is that life is God's gift to us. Life is short. Life is not always fair. But it is a gift. And we have the opportunity to use that gift to be the best that we can be. We have the opportunity to love, to care, to help each person with whom we come in contact and the opportunity to live as

Jesus taught us.

How we use our gift is our choice. Chris chose to use his gift to teach us and enrich our lives with his love, strength, and courage. And with God's help I hope I choose to live the same way."

Chris's death affected John so deeply that a year later John asked for a four-month leave of absence from work, so that he could explore and deal with everything that his loss had brought to the surface. The soul searching led him to question and to reevaluate his life and career in the light of what really mattered to him. Within two years he left his job, and returned to school for five more years to earn a Doctor of Psychology degree. His remarks follow.

"When I set out to share how Chris's illness and death affected my life, I thought that it would be relatively easy. In graduate school I completed an assignment that examined my spiritual growth, the content of which focused on my spiritual development in light of Chris's death. I fully expected, with some modification, to relay the same story. However, as I began writing this story, I found myself needing to talk about more than my spirituality because my graduate school assignment did not capture the full extent of how my life has changed since Chris died. As I took a step back from my writing, I knew that I could not say everything I needed to say in the space of this book. And the challenge for me would be to communicate very deep felt experiences and emotions in a very limited space.

I have a number of Chris's personal items. I went through them before writing this piece and one of the things I came across was a post card I sent him when I was living in London during the Fall of 1985. The last two lines of the post card referred to what we thought at the time were kidney stones. Immediately I began to relive Chris's illness. I know family members say they don't remember all of the details surrounding his illness and that they even have gaps around time and dates. Not me. I remember everything that I experienced, probably because, for me, every day felt like a year: the waiting, not knowing, hoping, feeling angry and helpless, desperate.

I knew that I wanted to spend every possible moment with him. I contemplated quitting my job but soon realized that wouldn't help matters. So I decided to come home every weekend, to spend time with Chris and my parents.

While struggling to cope with his illness, I never took the time to think about what my life would be like without Chris. I was so busy trying to keep my life together; I was afraid if I stopped to really think about the events of our lives, I would fall apart, physically and emotionally. As a result, I did not want to talk about Chris's illness and impending death. I did not feel that I was in denial because I was spending so much time with him. Yet, in retrospect, I had shut down all sense of feeling, something that I had become very good at over the years. My friends tried to support me, and the few that I let in have remained my closest friends. They didn't push me to think or feel; they just wanted to make sure I knew I wasn't alone. They would give me a similar response later in life.

After Chris's death I felt a deep sense of loneliness, missing my brother whom I loved very much. I missed being an older brother and was jealous of my male friends who still had their brothers. My success at work did not make my life any easier. I thought that once I received the important promotion I could relax and settle into a relationship and begin to enjoy life. But that didn't happen. Despite all of the material comforts I had achieved, I was miserable. I realize now that all of the things with which I surrounded myself were attempts to deny and ignore what I felt inside. I eventually quit my job hoping to find some answers to my pain.

Growing up in a conservative, Catholic family, I developed what I can now call an inflexible worldview. I had closed myself off to anything that challenged my perspective, which over time limited my growth and development. It also served to protect me from being hurt. Yet I did not think I was inflexible. I saw it as having planned out my life in a way that would allow me to live the life I always wanted. Chris's death forced me to confront the fact that life is not exact and predictable. As his illness progressed, I saw Chris adapt, dropping one set of goals and developing others that fit within his physical ability. When it became apparent that he would not be able to return to school, he set out to start a home publishing business. When he could no longer stay seated in a chair to work at the computer, he moved on to other interests that fit his physical range and stamina. His emotional resilience amazed me and made me feel inadequate because he moved through this stage of his life with such dignity, making the most out of his life.

My experience helped me to understand that I could experience deep pain and survive. In the past, I had always avoided putting my self in potentially painful experiences. I could not avoid Chris's death, and as a result learned a very powerful lesson. What I needed to learn next was how to put myself in situations that were avoidable, but necessary to live authentically.

Trying to move on with my life, I volunteered at pediatric cancer camps and a bereavement program at a local children's hospital. During this time, I came across a poem, the source of which I am unfamiliar, that put words to my experience:

Never let there be a time
When I cannot feel the pain,
When joy and sadness are blocked out
And only numbness reigns,

At least with pain I am alive
But numbness will destroy,
For if I cannot feel the pain
Then I cannot feel the joy.
(Author Unknown)

Eighteen years ago I was closed off from the world, not wanting to feel the pain associated with living my life authentically. Chris's illness and death shook me to the core, forcing me to re-examine how I lived my life. Allowing myself to truly feel the loss and pain associated with his death, and survive, I found myself willing to open myself to life's possibilities.

In hindsight, I realize that my quitting my job for graduate school was the beginning of my coming out process. I was slowly jettisoning the aspects of myself that I thought people wanted me to be and allowed my true self to grow. The result has astonished me. I am now in the loving relationship I had always wanted; and Doug and I are in the process of expanding our family through adoption. My family and friends have embraced us, which strengthens our relationship and my

decision to live my life for me and not others. A friend once told me that I was strongest when I was my most vulnerable. Watching Chris accept and live his life without complaint and regret, gave me the strength to do the same.

Also helping me live a full life is the knowledge that Chris is still with me. Throughout points in my life when I faced an important decision, I have felt a strong connection with Chris. When I was applying to graduate school, I was still not one hundred percent sure if it was the right move. I had received a counter offer from my employer to move to a new position, one that would require very little travel and move me to a higher salary. While I was debating my decision, I received my acceptance letter to school. The letter came on the anniversary of Chris's death. This and

other events have given me a strong connection to Chris
and my memories of our life together.
I am no longer jealous of my friends' relationship with
their brothers because I realize now that I still have my
relationship with Chris. It's just on a different level. While
our time together was short, it was very powerful and filled
with such fun: the Saturday morning adventures in the
woods, rafting the creek, building our train set, golfing, and
boating. I can still hear his voice when Chris wanted to get
my attention, John. . . . John. . . . John. I think of these
things often and take great joy in the love we shared and
continue to share throughout our lives."

Christopher nurtured us as much as we nurtured him. He
worried about what would happen to us after he was gone. He
hoped Michele would accept his death, and Maryann would
someday be able to finish her residency. He wanted me to get
on with my life and to finish the masters program. We have
respected his wish for us. We've all moved on with our lives.
We have made changes in our attitudes, our values and beliefs,
how we live in the world.

Michele has chosen to put her marriage to Steve, and her
spiritual and personal growth before her business career. In her
community, she provides many services for the soup kitchens
and serves on a regional, non-denominational board that raises
money to fund programs to feed the hungry.

Jack has retired from obstetrical practice; and now volunteers
his time at the Open Door Health Center. He serves on both
the local and regional Ethics Committees for a Catholic Order
that manages a number of hospitals in the mid-west. He is a
loving husband and father, and a caring grandfather who is
involved in our grandchildren's activities.

Maryann returned to finish her residency and is now practic-
ing. Her reputation is growing as a holistic physician who is
concerned not only for the body but also for the spirit. She

1) Chris, 20, on right acting in a play at Wabash College, 1983; 2) Chris, 20, the photographer being photographed, Wabash, 1983; 3) Chris, 21, Jack's birthday. Top left: Chris, Maryann, Michele. Bottom left: John, Jack, Therese, 1984.

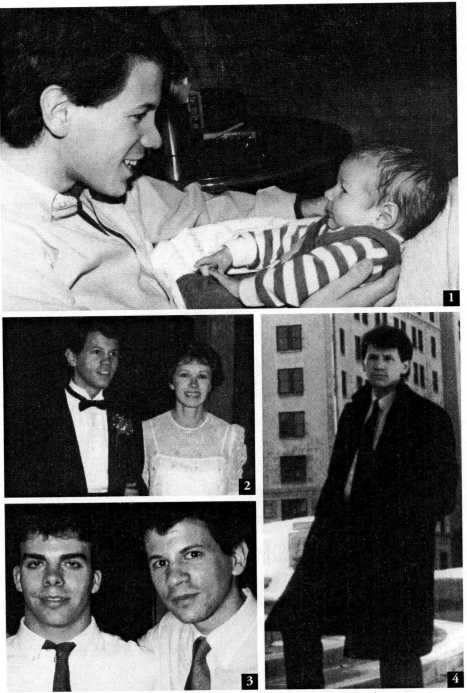

1) Chris with nephew, David, the weekend before surgery, 1986; 2) Chris, 21, accompanying Therese down the aisle at Maryann's wedding, 1985; 3) Chris, 21, at a fraternity-related event in Indianapolis, 1984; 4) Chris shortly after surgery with close friend, Mark, 1986.

The last photograph of Chris — taken in Florida in May, 1986.

13

CHRISTOPHER'S LEGACY

Chris has been and still is our teacher and catalyst. We learned so much from the experience of knowing, loving, and caring for him. It took his illness and death to awaken us to what is really important in this life: namely how to love and how to live. It took his imminent death to force us to look at the core issues of the meaning of life, and the meaning of death.

As painful as those last months were for all of us, they were a gift that Chris gave us: the last months of his life. I believe this was soul work for all of us. It was precious time that we had together, during which we got to know each other on a deeper level, and in the process of going through the pain and suffering, each of us changed and grew. We began to respond in more loving ways – from our higher selves rather than from ego.

As I reflected on the months that I took care of Chris, I became aware that each of us had been given whatever we needed to get through each day; whether it was courage, patience, understanding, resourcefulness, perseverance, kindness or wisdom. We were not doing it alone; rather God's grace nourished us as we endured the daily hardships, and attempted to live each day the best way we could. He gave us everything we needed when we needed it. Certainly Chris received the grace that he needed each day. And so did the rest of us. Besides spiritual help, we were given the strength to carry on. Jack, despite his personal grief and sadness, had to function at a very high level so that he would be able to perform early morning surgery, deliver babies at all hours, and make sound medical decisions. Each of our children had to carry on with the demands of the day, even though they would rather have stayed at Chris's side.

For the seven and one half months that Chris was at home, I helped either the nurse or Jack to lift and turn Chris every three to four hours, day and night. Although I frequently have lower back pain, and I can easily strain a muscle doing simple gardening work, I never had back pain during those months I helped to lift Chris. Even though I was not getting enough sleep, and I was emotionally and physically stressed, I only caught one cold and, atypically, it was completely gone the next morning.

Many evenings, especially toward the end of Chris's illness, I would be exhausted. I'd think, "I can't be too tired to take care of Chris. Take care of it, Lord." The tired feeling would quickly pass, and I would have enough energy to stay up with Chris for our nightly talks. It seemed to me that when my energy was at low ebb, I received more from the unlimited, universal Source. I try to remember that God continues to provide whatever I need each day. If He provides for me, He provides for everyone. Knowing and trusting that God provides makes life easier.

Being open to Chris about the truth of his condition, and being emotionally available to him and to each other, strengthened our love for one another, helped us to endure, brought us closer together, and as individuals and as a family, we became more supportive and nurturing.

Watching Chris let go of everything that he held dear in the physical world gave us the courage to let go of aspects of our own lives that no longer served us. Working through the pain of Chris's illness and death freed us from a lot of fear. Things that would have previously seemed insurmountable are no longer difficult to do. Very few trials would ever be as difficult as watching our son and brother suffer and die.

I'm learning to let go of fear as I listen to, trust, and follow my intuition. When I do, I make decisions that are good and ones with which I can live. I am willing to take the risk of standing up for what I believe even if it means criticism. This has been a big step for me.

One of the biggest fears it has eliminated is the fear of dying.

In helping Chris to face his fears about death and the next life, I was able to work through mine. The only thing we lose is our human body. It is not so much a leaving as a returning to. Our spirit continues. Death is simply a transition from this life into the higher life of spirit without losing those we have loved and left behind. Death is no longer frightening; it is simply the next step for our spirit.

We don't live in a random universe. Everything that happens to us has purpose. Looking back I realize that the graduate program I entered a year and a half before Chris's cancer was detected was exactly the type of experiential program that I needed, because it provided the means and the insight that I would need to take care of Chris. Because of this background, I responded to Chris in ways that would never otherwise have occurred to me. I became aware of the importance of Chris being involved in decision making and treatment plans, and his need to be in control of his life as much as possible. Along with learning counseling skills, journal writing, self-awareness, and personal growth were encouraged. These prepared me to respond to Chris's needs and later were instrumental in enabling me to write this book about our family journey. It was not a lucky choice on my part, a coincidence; I believe I was guided into the program. C. G. Jung would call it synchronicity, which recently I heard defined as "God wishing to remain anonymous!"

Without the counseling background I don't believe that I would have known that it was important for Jack and I to be emotionally open and available to Chris so that he would not feel isolated and alone. Throughout Chris's illness, Jack was compassionate and loving toward Chris. We didn't try to block our pain by putting up emotional walls. We went through the pain, our own and Chris's, and in so doing I feel that Chris, Jack, our children and I walked the journey together, and after his death, what we had shared together drew us closer. If we had not allowed ourselves to be emotionally vulnerable, I don't believe that we would have developed the close bond that we did.

I believe that all the positive energy sent to us through the prayers of so many concerned and loving people helped Chris and all of us to endure and grow emotionally and spiritually. The prayers did not heal Chris physically because recovery was not part of Chris's life plan. But once said and released, the prayers nurtured and supported us. As individuals and as a family we were sorely challenged, and we could have fallen apart. Then the journey might have led to bitterness and loss of faith, alienation from one another, and perhaps even divorce. The prayers helped us to get through our ordeal not by the skin of our teeth, but at a higher level: with love, involvement and commitment. Through grace and prayers and the program to which I was led, we received the strength and wisdom to respond to Chris and to each other in a more nurturing manner.

Chris's visits are incredible gifts for which I am most grateful and I know that he is often near. But there are still times when I pine for the physical Chris. I think if only I could hear his voice just once. I think that especially when I hear friends complain that their children don't visit often enough or stay long enough. Then I think to myself, "I would be happy simply hearing Chris's voice for one minute from the other side of the earth. Why are these people complaining?" This insight has made me more generous with my children. Jack and our children also feel that way, because we appreciate and enjoy the time that we do have together without complaining that it is not enough.

Chris's death was an end and a beginning. It was the end of a family who trusted and believed that medicine could cure all of our medical problems. As a medical family we were taught humility because medicine could not keep our brother and son alive.

As we were confronted with the imminent death of our beloved Chris, we were challenged to look beyond cure to the ultimate concerns of life and death. In our own way each of us began to search for the meaning that life and death held for us.

It was the beginning of a need and a desire to live authentically, intuitively, with greater spiritual awareness, and to remember that life is a beautiful gift from our creator. The greatest gifts are those we take for granted: the ability to give and receive love, the freedom to experience and enjoy the beauty of nature, the grace to walk, to be free of pain, to care for one's self. These are not prerogatives, they're gifts that we must appreciate and never take for granted.

Even when one is as limited as Chris was by his circumstances, he still had the freedom to make many choices. He chose his own medical treatment, where to live, how to live, whom to see, when to eat and sleep, whom to leave his worldly possessions to, how to respond to all of his caregivers, how to show love, and whether to address his fears about dying and to seek answers to his spiritual concerns.

We were called to forgive ourselves, each other, and the past. Forgive our physician friend for his missed diagnosis. Forgive each other and ourselves for not insisting that Chris get another medical opinion in October when the pain first began. Forgive ourselves for not being able to help our son and brother to get well.

Chris was another Christ in our lives. He was instrumental in causing us to shed our false selves. He drew us into a deeper spiritual life, greater love for God and for each other, and a commitment to live more fully in that love.

I am learning that joy and wisdom come, not through possession, but through opening ourselves to life and to love. Jack Kornfield, states in, *A Path With Heart,* that we are, "Called to let go and to allow the changing mystery of life to move through us." The challenge is to live through the changes in life without fear, without holding and grasping but with grace, wisdom and compassion.

I'm convinced that to help our loved one to die with dignity surrounded by love, is not the least we can do. It's the most we can do. Openly facing the issues that Chris's illness brought to the surface, has been one of the keys to coping, not only with Chris's illness, but also with our resulting separation and loss.

This life is our proving ground, our place of soul-making. Even though it's an interim place, what we learn here, how we grow and evolve here matters. From a humanistic standpoint, what we are and do and become here is important for the further development of the human race. But, beyond that, and most important to us as individuals, what we learn, and how we have grown by the end of this life, I believe determines the extent to which we are able to participate in the next life, the higher life of the spirit.

We learned so much about life, love, and eternity through the journey that we took with Christopher. It has been a sad journey that started with pain, anger, and fear; and ended with death, loss and separation. But the journey led us into a deeper love and appreciation for each other, a renewed sense of purpose, desire for spiritual growth, greater awareness and love of God, and a greater appreciation for the life that awaits us.

Journal Entry • December 31, 1999
Happy 36th Birthday Chris,

A special day! Your birthday and New Years Eve, 1999! Today my thoughts are filled with memories of you - good memories, happy memories, Chris. Twelve years ago I would never have thought that I could stop grieving. But I have, knowing that we never lost you. Your visits bring us such joy, and affirm over and over again that our love for one another will never end. I think at times you come just to say "Hi, I'm here." But at other times you seem to know when we need you, because you make your presence known during significant moments as though to support and assure us that you love us and are here for us. I am so thankful that I am allowed to know this, because I have a better understanding of the interconnectedness between those still in human form and our loved ones who have made the transition. I no longer feel sorry for you or for us because I know that your life, and so our lives, went as planned and was complete. In twenty-three years you accomplished what you had set out to learn in Earth School, and so you were able to move forward in the evolvement of your beautiful soul.

I'm so grateful that I'm a part of your life plan and that you're a pivotal part of mine and thankful for each moment that we had together. When I reflect on our last year and a half, especially the last seven and a half months when you were paralyzed, I perceive it as a time of grace for all of us. Through your pain and suffering to which I believe you said yes in that pre-earth moment, we grew and moved to a new level of understanding. And somewhere during the pain and suffering – yours and mine– I received a gift – I learned that God loves me.

Even though I miss you, I'm at peace because I know that you are experiencing joy and love beyond my comprehension. In this moment in time and in eternity – all is as it should be. You still "want to make things better" and I assure you that you do as you continue to bless and participate in our lives.

Chris, at Mass we sing a hymn titled, Here I Am Lord.

I, the Lord of Sea and Sky
I have heard my people cry
All who dwell in dark and sin my hand will save
I who made the stars at night
I will make their darkness bright
Who will bear my light to them?
Whom shall I send?
Here I am Lord
Is it I Lord?
I have heard you calling in the night.
I will go Lord,
If you lead me.
I will hold your people in my heart.

When I hear these words I think of you and the impact you had and continue to have on us. I think of you as the volunteer who offered to come to bear God's light to us because you did exactly that and lit up our lives with love. Thank you for all you did and continue to do for all of us. We are all meant to be volunteers bearing God's light to one another. How we succeed is up to each of us.

Chris, I feel blessed to be part of this family, to have kind, loyal friends, and a home on the lake you loved where we can all nurture our souls. I'm content and my life is full. Now, my life is about exploration — of ideas, of new ways of being, of insights, and of healing. Most of the time I feel centered and serene and find myself accepting life as it unfolds. I'm learning that each stage of life calls for courage, resilience, endurance, and above all faith. It requires a deep sense of our true nature. Real joy comes from living consciously, enjoying or at least accepting whatever each moment brings. The ideal, is to consciously live each moment on the human plane while also being aware of the other reality - that in which our spirit also participates. I remind myself that just as fish are surrounded by water, so we are surrounded by God. I wish I had a deeper awareness of God present in each moment. If I could do that then each moment would be full and perfect.

I think I finally understand the purpose, the reason for all life —to grow spiritually - to grow in love. I think I now understand that if I clear away all my fears, and if I let go of past hurts, anger, doubt, envy, and on and on, underneath it all is the only thing that I need to know — that the core of my being is love. So my focus is to give and to receive love. When I judge others, I'm filtering them and their statements and actions through my wounded self. I love knowing this! Life becomes easier, simpler. I think that's what we struggle to learn. Not knowing this is what keeps us feeling separated from God and from each other. When we focus on love, there is no separation. Then, whatever we do, big or small, "insignificant" or not, if it is done out of love, not fear, then we are joined with Stillpoint, our Creator, and with all of life.

✂ BIBIOGRAPHY ✂

Anderson, Joan Webster. *Where Angels Walk.* Sea Cliff: Barton & Brett, Publishers, Inc., 1992.

Benson, Herbert, and Klipper, Miriam Z. *The Relaxation Response.* New York: Avon, 1975.

Bolen, Jean Shinoda. *The Tao of Psychology.* San Francisco: Harper and Row, 1979.

Brinkly, Dannion with Perry, Paul. *At Peace In The Light.* New York: Harper Collins Publishers, Inc., 1995.

De Mello, Anthony. *Awareness.* New York: Doubleday, 1990.

Dolan, James R. SJ. *Meditations for Life.* Syracuse: Scotsman Press, 1991.

Elliott, William. *Tying Rocks to Clouds.* New York: Doubleday, 1996.

Esko, Wendy. *Macrobiotic Cooking for Everyone.* Tokyo: Japan Publications, 1980.

Fox, Matthew. *Original Blessing.* New York: Tarcher Putnam, 1983.

Grassi, Dominic. *Bumping Into God.* Chicago: Loyola Press, 1999.

Hurnard, Hannah. *Hinds' Feet on High Places.* Wheaton: Tyndale House Publishers, Inc., 1975.

Kalish, Richard. *Death, Grief, and Caring Relationships.*
Monterey: Brooks/Cole Publishing, 1981.

Kubler-Ross, Elisabeth. *Death: The Final Stage of Growth.*
Englewood Cliffs: Prentice-Hall, Inc., 1975.

Kubler-Ross, Elisabeth. *On Death and Dying.* New York:
McMillan Publishing Company Inc., 1969.

Jampolsky, Gerald G. *Teach Only Love.* Toronto: Bantam
Books, 1983.

Matthews-Simonton, Stephanie, Simonton, Carl O., and
Creighton, James L. *Getting Well Again.* Toronto:Bantam
Book, 1980.

Moody, Raymond A. *Life After Life.* Toronto: Bantam Books,
1975.

Moody, Raymond A. *Reflections on Life After Life.* Toronto:
Bantam Books, 1977.

Moody, Raymond A. with Perry, Paul.Reunions *Visionary
Encounters With Departed Loved Ones.* New York: Villard
Books, a division of Random House, Inc., 1993.

Moore, Thomas. *Care Of The Soul.* New York: Harper
Perennial, 1992.

Mother Teresa. Compiled by Jose Luis Gonzales-Balado.
In My Own Words. New York: Gramercy Books, a division of
Random House Value Publishing, Inc., 1996

Mother Teresa. *Thirsting For God.* Compiled by Fr. Angelo
Scolozzi, M.C.III.O. Ann Arbor: Servant Publications., 1999.

Myss, Caroline. Sacred Contracts *Awakening Your Divine Potential.* New York: Three Rivers Press, a division of Random House, Inc., 2002.

Nicholl, Donald. *Holiness.* New York: Paulist Press, 1981.

Peck, Rosalie, and Stefanics, Charlotte. *Learning To Say Goodbye.* Muncie: Accelerated Development, Inc., 1987.

Puryear, Anne. *Stephen Lives!* New York: Pocket Books, a division of Simon & Schuster Inc., 1992.

Sattilaro, Anthony J. *Recalled By Life.* New York: Avon, 1982

Six, Jean-Francois. *Light of the Night The Last Eighteen Months in the Life of Therese Of Lisieux.* Notre Dame: University of Notre Dame Press, 1998

Tubesing, Donald A. *Kicking Your Stress Habits.* New York: American Library, 1981.

Van Praagh, James. *Talking To Heaven.* New York: Penguin Group, Penguin Putnam Inc., 1997.

Van Praagh, James. *Reaching To Heaven.* New York: Penguin Group, Penguin Putnam Inc., 1999.

Upson, Norma S. *When Someone You Love Is Dying.* New York: Simon and Shuster, 1986.

Worden, William J. *Grief Counseling and Grief Therapy.* Boston: Houghton Mifflin Company, 1978.

Zukav, Gary. *The Seat of The Soul.* New York: Simon & Schuster, 1989.